COUNTDOWN
TO THE
APOCALYPSE

COUNTDOWN
TO THE
APOCALYPSE

LEARN TO READ THE SIGNS THAT
THE LAST DAYS HAVE BEGUN

GRANT R. JEFFREY

WaterBrook
PRESS

COUNTDOWN TO THE APOCALYPSE
PUBLISHED BY WATERBROOK PRESS
12265 Oracle Boulevard, Suite 200
Colorado Springs, Colorado 80921
A division of Random House Inc.

Scripture quotations are taken from the King James Version.

Italics in Scripture quotations indicate the author's added emphasis.

ISBN 978-1-4000-7441-9

Library of Congress Cataloging-in-Publication Data
Jeffrey, Grant R.
    Countdown to the Apocalypse : learn to read the signs that the last days have begun / Grant R. Jeffrey. — 1st ed.
        p. cm.
    Includes bibliographical references (p.   ).
    ISBN 978-1-4000-7441-9
    1. Bible—Prophecies—End of the world. 2. End of the world—Biblical teaching.
3. Bible—Prophecies—Second Advent. 4. Second Advent—Biblical teaching. I. Title.
    BS649.E63J45 2008
    236'.9—dc22

                                        2008024105

Printed in the United States of America
2008—First Edition

10 9 8 7 6 5 4 3 2 1

SPECIAL SALES
Most WaterBrook Multnomah books are available in special quantity discounts when purchased in bulk by corporations, organizations, and special interest groups. Custom imprinting or excerpting can also be done to fit special needs. For information, please e-mail SpecialMarkets@WaterBrookPress.com or call 1-800-603-7051.

Contents

Contents

Acknowledgments

Countdown to the Apocalypse is the result of more than four decades of extensive, detailed research into the history, archaeology, and prophecies of the book of Daniel. In my lifelong study of Daniel's prophecies, I have acquired more than three hundred books—written by both Jewish and Christian scholars—that examine Daniel's predictions. Daniel's unique life and blameless character, as well as his unwavering faithfulness to God and His people, have been an inspiration to me.

As this book will demonstrate, we are now witnessing the fulfillment of numerous unique prophecies that are setting the stage for the return of Jesus Christ in our lifetime. Jesus encouraged believers to have no fear but rather to be filled with the hope of our coming redemption when we see the fulfillment of these prophecies. He declared, "And when these things begin to come to pass, then look up, and lift up your heads; for your redemption draweth nigh" (Luke 21:28).

My parents inspired me through their faith, their deep commitment to Jesus Christ, and their lifelong interest in the Scriptures' prophecies of Christ's Second Coming.

I dedicate *Countdown to the Apocalypse* to my loving wife, Kaye. She continues to inspire my writing as well as being my faithful partner in my research, archaeological explorations, and writing ministry. Her constant encouragement and practical assistance enabled me to complete this important manuscript.

Acknowledgments

I trust that my biblical research will inform, inspire, and encourage you to personally study the deep meaning of the prophecies of Daniel, the greatest prophet of the Old Testament.

Grant R. Jeffrey
Toronto, Ontario
February 2008

The Babylon Prophecy

B ABYLON, BOTH AS A LEGENDARY ANCIENT CITY and the first unrivaled world empire, has loomed large in memory throughout human history. Six hundred years before Jesus came to earth, the Euphrates River Valley was home to the magnificent Babylonian Empire. The Babylonians had conquered the rest of the known world and brought untold numbers of people from the defeated kingdoms to Babylon as slaves.

Among the slaves was a young man who was chosen by God to become one of the greatest of the Hebrew prophets. God gave Daniel visions of the future and the ability to interpret dreams. While living in exile, Daniel recorded prophecies that some twenty-six centuries later give us a highly detailed look at our own future. Daniel saw the unfolding of human history and the days of Jesus Christ on earth. And as we will read in the chapters that follow, he saw the most detailed visions describing the end of the age—the days that we are about to enter.

We live in prophetic times, so it is not surprising that the land of Babylon—present-day Iraq and parts of present-day Iran—is the focus of international tension and the subject of daily news reports. Iraq is torn by violent insurgencies, armed factions fighting for control of the country, and sectarian violence that continually causes injury and death. Foreign fighters, devoted to the cause of Al Qaeda and radical Islam, enter Iraq to join militant groups, to help train terrorists, to battle against Western allied forces, and to plot the demise of the State of Israel.

THE POWER OF ANCIENT BABYLON

The name Babylon still evokes a powerful image of the greatest city of the ancient world. The name is derived from *babel,* a Hebrew word meaning "the gate of God." Located fifty-six miles south of modern-day Baghdad in Iraq, it rapidly grew in power until it became the most important city in the ancient world. Babylon is in an area originally known by the name Sumer, or Shinar, designating the fertile country lying between the Tigris and Euphrates rivers. The land also was known as Mesopotamia, meaning "the land between the rivers."

The first mention of Babylon in the Bible reveals that the city of Babel was founded by Nimrod, who was the son of Cush. "Cush begat Nimrod: he began to be a mighty one in the earth. He was a mighty hunter before the LORD.... And the beginning of his kingdom was Babel" (Genesis 10:8–10). This was the site of the first widespread rebellion against God. The men of Babel built an enormous tower in an arrogant attempt to rebel against God and make themselves famous. "And they said, Go to, let us build us a city and a tower, whose top may reach unto heaven; and let us make us a name, lest we be scattered abroad upon the face of the whole earth" (Genesis 11:4). God's response was to "confound their language, that they may not understand one another's speech" (Genesis 11:7). In the confusion that resulted, "the LORD scattered them abroad from thence upon the face of all the earth: and they left off to build the city" (Genesis 11:8). Scientists have verified the dispersion of humanity throughout three continents after the Flood (see Genesis 10:32; 11:8–9).

History records that much later, around 1760 BC, King Hammurabi made Babylon the political and religious capital of his very powerful but small empire. Hammurabi combined astute diplomacy with superb military leadership to defeat the surrounding kingdoms in Mesopotamia. He was the first major king who created a written code of laws, known as the Code of Hammurabi. He became the ruler of the first united Babylonian Empire, which extended from the Persian Gulf to the Habur River more than a millennium before the rise of the Babylonian Empire of Nebuchadnezzar.

In the seventh century BC, under King Nabopolassar and later his famous son, Nebuchadnezzar, the new empire of Babylon waged continuous wars against neighboring kingdoms, laying waste to cities and carrying countless numbers of people into captivity. Most notable among the millions of captives were the Judeans of Israel, who were taken in three phases between 606 BC and 587 BC.

Some historical sources conclude that Nebuchadnezzar conquered Judah in 605 BC. However, a careful reading of the Scriptures reveals that the correct date is actually 606 BC. The prophet Jeremiah recorded, "The word that came to Jeremiah concerning all the people of Judah in the fourth year of Jehoiakim the son of Josiah king of Judah, that was the first year of Nebuchadrezzar king of Babylon" (Jeremiah 25:1). Jehoiakim's "fourth year" was 605 BC. However, Daniel declared that Jerusalem was taken by Nebuchadnezzar's army a year earlier, in the "third year of the reign of Jehoiakim king of Judah" (Daniel 1:1), which was the year 606 BC. The historian Henry Fynes Clinton also confirmed in his exhaustive chronological study of ancient history that Prince Nebuchadnezzar led his army against the kingdom of Judah in the summer of 606 BC.[1]

The Babylonian Empire did not endure for long, however. The Medo-Persian Empire, led by the powerful kings Darius and Cyrus the Great, conquered the empire and the city of Babylon in 538 BC. But in the years that Nebuchadnezzar ruled the known world, God raised up Daniel, one of Israel's greatest prophets.

DANIEL'S VISION OF OUR FUTURE

While serving in Babylon's royal courts, Daniel saw remarkable visions and interpreted inspired dreams. Many of his visions foretold the upheaval in the world that came to pass more than two thousand years ago. In fact, the fulfillment of those prophecies verifies that Daniel was truly God's prophet. His predictions came true exactly as they were given. However, many of Daniel's most intriguing prophecies describe events that are still to come. The generation that you and I are part of will see the fulfillment of these last-days prophecies.

In this book we will examine all of Daniel's prophecies—the ones that were fulfilled long ago and those that are soon to be fulfilled. Our generation will witness the rise of the Antichrist and the False Prophet, the Tribulation period, the Antichrist's political and military domination of the world, the battle of Armageddon, and the return to earth of Jesus Christ.

A bas-relief sculpture of King Cyrus the Great of Persia

Daniel's ancient Babylonian prophecies give us a precise time line that reveals the sequence of events and the amount of time that will separate the major developments of the last days. It is certain that the events Daniel described will occur during the current generation.

If you know what to look for, you will see that signs of the last days are appearing all around us. I invite you to join me in this study of Daniel's prophecies. Together we will discover what the future holds for God's people as well as for those who wage war against God.

Chapter 1

Opening the Sealed Vision from Babylon

The Future That Daniel Described Is Now

But thou, O Daniel, shut up the words,
and seal the book, even to the time of the end.

—DANIEL 12:4

Blessed is he that readeth, and they that hear
the words of this prophecy, and keep those things
which are written therein: for the time is at hand.

—REVELATION 1:3

J ESUS CHRIST, THE GREATEST OF ALL THE PROPHETS, prepared His followers to be able to read the signs of the times. Jesus pointed out that, in the midst of world upheaval, it is necessary to understand the meaning of key developments. Speaking to His disciples, Jesus described the events that would signal the final countdown to the Apocalypse. He wanted His followers to be prepared for the revealing of Christ at the end of the age.

In His own prophecy, Jesus referred to a revelation from Daniel's vision (see Matthew 24:15; Daniel 9:24–27). As we will see later in this chapter, Daniel's words—repeated hundreds of years later by Jesus—serve as a crucial guide as we attempt to understand the signs of our times. Jesus walked the earth some five centuries after Daniel recorded his prophecies. But both

Jesus and Daniel looked ahead through time to our generation as they described the events that will lead to the final battle between God and Satan. Jesus' prophetic message in Matthew 24 had a recurring theme: be prepared!

Jesus was careful to give us the information we need to understand the times we live in and to prepare our hearts for what lies just ahead. He said we should look for certain prophetic developments as they unfold, and He called our attention to Daniel's vision: "When ye therefore see the abomination of desolation, spoken of by Daniel the prophet, stand in the holy place, (whoso readeth, let him understand:)" (Matthew 24:15). By quoting Daniel's prophecy about the Antichrist defiling the rebuilt Temple in Jerusalem, Jesus gave the Hebrew prophet His divine seal of approval. Second only to Jesus Christ, Daniel stands as God's greatest prophet. His words will guide and enlighten us as we study his prophecies and learn to identify the events that will characterize the end of this age. Jesus points us to Daniel because He wants us to be spiritually prepared for the challenges that lie just ahead.

THE RISE OF THE ANTICHRIST

As history rushes toward the culmination of the current age, it's important that we recognize the signposts that point to hidden events and trends that are only hinted at in news headlines. Daniel's prophecies show that what is happening in Europe, the Middle East, and parts of Asia today are clear warnings of what will occur tomorrow. Daniel gave us a precise time line that plots the sequence of major end-time developments. Many of the events that are specified on his time line have already occurred.

Daniel foretold the unfolding of ancient human history, including the four great empires that controlled the known world for more than two thousand years. Daniel's vision of the seventy weeks describes sixty-nine "weeks" of years, leading up to the crucifixion of Christ. The time of Christ's life on earth, and His death and resurrection, is followed by a gap between the sixty-ninth and seventieth weeks of years. It is during this gap that the church has been spreading the Christian faith throughout the world.

Today we are approaching the commencement of the seventieth week of Daniel's vision. In preparation for this final phase of Daniel's prophetic time line, the world witnessed the return of the Jews from thousands of years of exile to their homeland. Prior to 1948, few people believed the Jews would ever realize their dream of once again occupying the Promised Land. After being scattered to the four corners of the earth, the Jews finally reestablished the State of Israel on May 15, 1948. Not only was it an answer to their ancient prayer of "next year in Jerusalem," but the creation of the nation of Israel signaled to those Christians who are familiar with biblical prophecy that Jesus Christ will return to earth in our generation.

The Jews' return to Palestine restarted the clock on the prophetic time line. Using the year 1948 as a critical starting point, we can now look for other major prophetic signs of what is to come. As we study Daniel's prophecies, we will note the end-times developments that are *already* under way in our generation.

Based on the information we have from God's prophets, it is very likely that the figure known as the Antichrist has already been born and is an adult living in Europe. We do not know the name of the Antichrist, but we do know that the name will somehow be connected with the mystical Hebrew/Greek number 666 (see Revelation 13:16–18). He will soon arise and become visible on the global scene. Those who are students of prophecy will know who he is at that time, because he will gradually position him-self as the politically unrivaled leader of the united Europe. Later he will take political control of the entire world. The generation alive today will see all these prophetic events develop. The Antichrist will consolidate all political, economic, and military power on a scale never before seen in human history. He will rise to rule the world through a confederation of European and Mediterranean nations. This is the prophesied revival of the ancient Roman Empire, which Daniel foretold.

Today Daniel's visions take on a much greater immediacy, because he was describing *our own time,* our generation. The future is now.

GOD IS PREPARING US FOR CHRIST'S RETURN

The Lord God is using Daniel's prophecies to prepare both Jewish and Christian believers for what lies ahead. As Jesus taught in the gospel of Matthew, we all need to be prepared for the future. In this book we will explore Daniel's prophecies that were fulfilled in ancient times, attesting to his credentials as a true prophet of God. We will also look at his prophe-cies that describe developments that are taking place in our own day and those that will come to pass in the very near future.

Here are just a few of the major developments that God's prophets have revealed will occur in our generation:

- The ancient Roman Empire will be revived in the last days and will become the power base of the kingdom of the Antichrist.
- The Antichrist will launch a political career that grows in influence and power. He will consolidate his economic, political, and mili-tary power in Europe, eventually becoming the unrivaled dictator of the world.

- He will make a seven-year treaty (a "covenant") with Israel, guaranteeing its security. This will prove to be a false treaty—in reality, a covenant with death.
- The Antichrist will be assassinated at the midpoint of the seven-year covenant and then will be brought back to life by the power of Satan. This is a satanic false parallel to the resurrection of Christ, and the satanic resurrection will deceive those who have not studied and understood the revelations of God's prophets.
- The Antichrist and his partner, the False Prophet, will orchestrate the implementation of the Mark of the Beast, a totalitarian police system whereby every person on earth will be tracked. Through the mechanism of the Mark of the Beast, closely associated with the number 666, every person will lose his or her privacy and personal freedom following the death and resurrection of the Antichrist. Those who accept the mark will acknowledge their spiritual submission to the Antichrist.
- The world will be plunged into a series of wars involving a number of devastating battles that lead to the cataclysmic battle of Armageddon, the war that will end this age.
- In the battle of Armageddon, the western nations of the revived Roman Empire that are loyal to the Antichrist will wage war against the enormous armies of the "kings of the east" (Revelation 16:12). The armies of the Antichrist will occupy Israel and the Middle East with overwhelming numbers of troops and vastly superior weaponry. Then a massive, two-hundred-million-man army will arise from Asia and will invade the Middle East. At that final conflict the battle of Armageddon will be fought in northern Israel in the Valley of Jezreel. The carnage and utter devastation of this war will be unprecedented.

- The battle of Armageddon will conclude with Jesus Christ's return to earth, when He comes to rescue His chosen people. He will defend Israel by defeating both the massive armies of the eastern and western enemy forces that will be arrayed in battle against God's people.
- Jesus Christ will defeat the Antichrist and banish Satan to the bottomless pit for a thousand years. Christ will then establish His messianic kingdom on earth.

THE EVENT THAT STARTS A NEW COUNTDOWN

For years prophecy teachers have tried to match Daniel's famous vision of the seventy weeks with a time line that adheres to the Western calendar. Such efforts failed to accurately correlate the prophetic time line with the modern system of measuring months and years. Many students of prophecy overlooked a crucial factor: the book of Daniel was written before the current Western calendar was created. In my studies of Daniel, I discovered that to accurately cross-reference his remarkably precise time descriptions with the modern calendar, I had to go back to the Hebrew biblical calendar. First, I used the ancient Hebrew calendar to measure the passage of prophetic years, with each year consisting of 360 days (twelve months of 30 days each). When reading Daniel's prophecy using the 360-day calendar, it is possible to determine the sequence of the major prophetic events during the future seven-year Tribulation period. One can also establish the precise passage of time in between these critical events. We will examine these issues in greater detail in chapter 8.

As we consider the sequence of last-days events that Daniel described, it's essential to note the one prophetic event that serves as a trigger for all that follows. The Antichrist will draw up a seven-year treaty, and Israel will enter into this covenant with death. Once the treaty is signed, a very specific series of events will unfold during the next seven years. The treaty referred to in Daniel 9:27 marks the beginning of a seven-year countdown to Christ's return, coinciding with the whole Tribulation period. Beginning with the signing of the treaty as day one of the seven-year Tribulation, we can calculate the number of days that will separate each of the major events of the Tribulation. We are able to determine when the Antichrist will put a stop to daily animal sacrifices on the Temple Mount in Jerusalem, when the Antichrist will desecrate the Temple, when the Antichrist will be assassinated and subsequently resurrected satanically, and when the final battle of Armageddon will conclude.

SIGNS OF THE FUTURE YOU CAN READ TODAY

While these events remain in the future, numerous developments are already putting in place the crucial components of the Antichrist's future rule. Daniel's prophecy points to the following developments, which are already under way.

The Revived Roman Empire

The leaders and bureaucrats of the United Kingdom, France, Italy, and Germany are working behind the scenes to unify Europe without calling for another vote on a European constitution. They lost the last vote decisively. Since then the political alliances of the elites have continued to advance without the informed approval of the people. The political elites are maneuvering to create an international coalition that will, in effect, restore the Roman Empire. In the absence of a full public debate, the leaders of key European nations have initiated the political and legal arrangements that will form a European superstate.

This action defies the wishes of a majority of the population in the European Union, in which citizens voting in national referendums rejected a proposed European constitution. However, without the people's informed consent, the elected (and many unelected) leaders of Europe continue to lay the groundwork for the "United States of Europe." To those who doubt that supporters of the new European Union intend to create the world's first superstate in Europe, they should consider the evidence. The enlarged European Union already meets the legal definition of an independent, sovereign state. The Montevideo Convention on the Rights and Duties of States—a treaty signed at Montevideo, Uruguay, in 1933—established the criteria that identify a sovereign state. The treaty declared that a state possesses these essential characteristics:

- a permanent population
- a defined territory
- a government
- the capacity to enter into relations with other states

The enlarged European Union possesses all these qualifications.

An Army Numbering Two Hundred Million Troops

China, India, and their Asian allies are positioned to raise a two-hundred-million-man army in the near future. This army can be marshaled to form the prophesied pan-Asian military force of the kings of the east, which will wage war in Israel against the armies of the Antichrist. What was impossible at any time in the past is now a real possibility.

Drying Up the Euphrates River

Daniel prophesied that the great Euphrates River (a historic military barrier between the east and the west) will dry up—something that has never happened. However, it is now possible following the construction of the huge Atatürk Dam in Turkey. This massive dam can cut off the flow of the headwaters of the Euphrates in the mountains of Turkey.

Advanced Genocidal Weapons Systems

Several nations now have access to a genetic weapon that kills victims selectively, based on their ethnicity. By acting selectively on a victim's DNA, Arabs, Jews, Asians, or Caucasians could be singled out for death on a massive scale. In a time of battle, or even by targeting certain civilian populations, an enemy force could commit unprecedented ethnic cleansing through the use of advanced genetic weapons.[1]

APOCALYPTIC WRITINGS

In his book, Daniel reveals that he saw God in an awesome vision. The prophet saw God in His glory as "the Ancient of days," sitting in judgment on all mankind (7:9). One of Daniel's major prophetic themes is that despite the appearance that evil is triumphing, God will ultimately judge both individual sinners and wicked nations. This certainty that God will set all things right will be crucial to the Tribulation believers who are living under the tyranny of the Antichrist.

The book of Daniel, the writings of Zechariah, the book of Revelation, and a portion of Isaiah's prophecies (chapters 24–27) are described by scholars as an "apocalypse." The Greek word for *apocalypse* means an "unveiling," the revelation of something that has previously been hidden.

Throughout the Word of God, the Lord inspired His prophets to create apocalyptic writings using figures of speech and prophetic symbols to reveal the events that will unfold during the climax of history. God has promised that in the last days Jesus will return as the promised Messiah. Only God knows the future and accurately reveals it to us. The Lord has made it clear that accurate prophecy is impossible unless He inspires a person to reveal future events (see Isaiah 46:9–10).

Since ancient times, Daniel has been numbered among the most highly regarded of God's prophets. The early Christian theologian Augustine wrote about "the testimony of the prophet Daniel, who most plainly foretold that the saints should receive the kingdom of the Most High."[2] Further, the Christian writer Jerome (AD 385) wrote of the importance of Daniel's writing, saying, "None of the prophets spoke so plainly of Christ."[3]

READING THE SIGNS OF YOUR FUTURE

God revealed the future to Daniel in ways that no other prophet was allowed to witness. Babylon had destroyed the kingdom of Judah, yet God chose a young Hebrew captive living in Babylon to observe and record detailed visions of the precise time of the first coming of Israel's Messiah, as well as the events that will lead to the Messiah's return to earth in the years to come.

In Daniel's prophecies, God revealed the precise timing of the key events of the last days. But Daniel's prophecies reveal far more than just the end of the age. The prophet's vision of the seventy weeks is a calendar of God's dealings with humanity, especially Israel, throughout history. Daniel describes the rise and fall of four Gentile empires that successively dominated the world. He also foretold the precise time that the leaders of Israel would reject their promised Messiah. Daniel prophesied the rise of the revived Roman Empire, which we see developing today. Daniel received astonishing visions from God that describe Satan's all-out war against God and His chosen people. Daniel also saw God's destruction of Satan through the power of His Son, Jesus Christ, the returning Messiah.

I believe that these events, foretold by Daniel more than twenty-five centuries in the past, will occur during our generation. While no one but God knows the actual day and time of Christ's return, God did reveal to the famous prophet of Babylon the signs that would show God's people they are living in the last generation. Those who have seriously studied Daniel's prophecy are now reading those signs.

THE TIME LINE FOR THE LAST DAYS

The rebirth of Israel in 1948 announced to students of Bible prophecy much more than simply the creation of a new nation. The long-awaited ingathering of Jews from more than seventy nations back to their ancient homeland signaled the start of God's prophetic countdown. Jesus revealed that the generation that was alive to see the rebirth of the nation of Israel would live to witness the final conflict between Jesus Christ and the forces of Satan at the battle of Armageddon (see Matthew 24:32–34).

In the years that have passed since the Jewish exiles returned to Israel, world events have moved rapidly toward the end of the age. Daniel pointed to significant political, military, and technological developments that are setting the stage for Christ's return. I will address these signs of the times in greater detail in chapters 10 and 11. The most evident signs on the world stage are the rebirth of Israel, the reappearance of the ancient Roman Empire, the Islamic and Russian preparations for an unprecedented genocidal war against Israel, the development of new weapons technology that makes possible the cataclysmic warfare described in Daniel's prophecy, and the development of advanced computer technology and a cashless society that will make it possible for the Antichrist to control not only governments but the lives of billions of individuals.

In chapter 8, we will look at Daniel's remarkable prophecies that were fulfilled to the very day nearly two thousand years ago with the rejection of Jesus Christ as Israel's Messiah. In chapters 3 and 6, we will examine prophecies about the destiny of the four Gentile world empires that have dominated human history for twenty-five hundred years during the "times of the Gentiles" (Luke 21:24). And in chapters 9, 10, and 11, we will study Daniel's prophecies that are yet to be fulfilled, regarding the nature of the Antichrist, the Mark of the Beast, the Tribulation, the unprecedented global war that will destroy the world political system as we know it, and the return of Christ to protect His people and destroy Satan. These are prophecies that will be fulfilled in our generation.

As we cross-reference ancient prophecy with major political-military developments taking place in our world today, two things become evident. First, God has not left biblically aware Christians unprepared. He has provided the necessary prophetic knowledge in advance of the unfolding events. The Lord commanded Daniel to record his visions so Jewish and Christian believers living in the last days would be able to read the signs of the end times. God has provided hope, insight, and encouragement that assure His followers that the troubling events in our days are setting the stage for the long-awaited return of Jesus Christ. Because of Daniel, we know that after the terrible days of the Tribulation period, Christ will return to defeat Satan and his armies. At that time Jesus Christ will establish His millennial rule on earth.

Chapter 2

The Greatest of God's Prophets

Daniel Described Your Future in Detail

The king Nebuchadnezzar fell upon his face,
and worshipped Daniel, and commanded
that they should offer an oblation
and sweet odours unto him.
The king answered unto Daniel, and said,
Of a truth it is, that your God is a God of gods,
and a Lord of kings, and a revealer of secrets,
seeing thou couldest reveal this secret.

—DANIEL 2:46–47

D ANIEL IS THE GREATEST OF THE ANCIENT PROPHETS of Israel, both in his
unblemished character as a man of God and in his unparalleled ability
to read the future. Of all the Old Testament prophets, Daniel provided
the most detailed description of the major events of the "time of the end"
(Daniel 12:9). The Jewish historian Flavius Josephus, a contemporary of
the apostle Paul, characterized Daniel's unique mission: "He not only predicted the future, like the other prophets, but specified when the events
would happen."[1]

The great physicist Sir Isaac Newton was so fascinated by Daniel's
prophecies that he wrote a book about the prophet. "To reject Daniel is to
reject the Christian religion," Newton wrote, indicating the fundamental

role these prophecies play in Christian thought.[2] The main themes of Christian eschatology were developed by the great Hebrew prophets, particularly Daniel and Ezekiel. Various New Testament prophecies (found especially in Matthew and Revelation) were derived from the prophetic themes found in the book of Daniel. Daniel heavily influenced the concepts and language of Zechariah and Haggai and the New Testament apostles Paul and John. The first-century Jewish Essene priests at the village of Qumran, near the Dead Sea, gave Daniel's prophecies the highest place of honor in both their theology and their studies focused on their messianic expectations.[3]

The prophetic expectations of generations of faithful Jews and Christians were shaped to a large degree by their understanding of the prophecies of Daniel.[4] And today, Daniel's visions continue to shape the prophetic hopes and concerns of millions of Jews and Christians.

DANIEL'S SERVICE IN A PAGAN ROYAL COURT

After Prince Nebuchadnezzar of Babylon conquered Judah in 606 BC, Daniel and three friends were part of the first group of exiles deported six hundred miles east to Babylon (see 2 Kings 24:1–2; Daniel 1:1). This was the first of three major deportations to Babylon. Daniel was descended from princely blood (see Daniel 1:3–6). Josephus declared that Daniel was descended from the family of King Zedekiah.[5] According to multiple sources, there also is evidence that Daniel was a descendant of King Jeconiah.[6]

We know more details about Daniel's private life, history, ancestry, and character than we know about any other prophet. When the aristocratic Jewish captives were taken in chains to Babylon, their names were changed, following the Babylonian custom, to demonstrate the absolute power of their conqueror. Daniel's Hebrew name meant "God is my judge." However, in Babylon it was changed to Belteshazzar, which meant "Bel's treasurer," in honor of Bel, the pagan god of Babylon. Daniel's friend Hananiah, whose Hebrew name meant "God is gracious to me," was renamed Shadrach, meaning "messenger of the sun." Mishael's Hebrew name, meaning "who is as God," was changed to Meshach, which meant "Who is like Venue?" Azariah's Hebrew name meant "the Lord helped" but was changed to Abednego, meaning "the servant of Nego," another of Babylon's gods.

It was the custom of the Babylonians to take captives from the best noble and royal families of conquered nations and train them as future advisors to the royal court. For three years captured members of noble families were taught all the knowledge, wisdom, and languages they would need to advise a Babylonian ruler. Libraries in Babylon held hundreds of thousands of documents inscribed on baked-clay tablets, and these documents were used to educate and train foreign students. Ultimately they became major court advisors to the kings of the greatest empire the ancient world had ever known.

Daniel and his friends were probably about sixteen years old when they were taken to Babylon. These captives were "children in whom was no blemish, but well favoured, and skilful in all wisdom" (Daniel 1:4). When Daniel and his companions were captured in Jerusalem, it is possible they were made eunuchs. Daniel 1:3 records that the prisoners were under the control of the master of the eunuchs, one of the key officials of the pagan kingdom, during the first three years of their training. The phrase "master of his eunuchs" clearly refers to the official who served as the chief of the king's special advisors. Many of the ancient royal courts in the Middle East used a group of officials, sometimes royal or noble captives from conquered nations, that were made eunuchs because the ancient kings believed that these men would then be able to focus their attention on their governmental duties rather than be concerned with a family.

While initially the word *eunuch* was exclusively used in ancient times to describe male captives who were surgically altered to prevent future reproductive activity, there is ample evidence from the history of this period that *eunuch* came to apply to all royal ministers and advisors. For example, the Jewish religious commentary *The Testimony of Joseph,* written during the intertestament period preceding the birth of Jesus, refers to the Egyptian official Potiphar using the title *eunuch,* despite the fact that Potiphar was a married father of children.[7]

Centuries earlier Isaiah foretold, "Of thy sons that shall issue from thee, which thou shalt beget, shall they take away; and they shall be eunuchs in the palace of the king of Babylon" (Isaiah 39:7). Josephus recorded, "He also made some of them to be eunuchs.… Now among these were four of the family of Zedekiah, of most excellent dispositions; the one of whom was called Daniel, another Ananias, another Misael, and the fourth Azarias; and the king of Babylon changed their names."[8]

Daniel was trained in all the wisdom of the pagan culture of Babylon, just as Moses had been trained almost a millennium earlier in the highest esoteric knowledge of ancient Egypt. Like Moses and Joseph, Daniel began his adult life as a slave with significantly fewer rights than an inmate in our worst prisons today. However, under the guidance of God, Daniel quickly rose from a slave to become the powerful prime minister in two world empires: first the empire of Babylon and then of Media-Persia. As a prophet, Daniel also was given the ability to interpret the dreams of others. Daniel interpreted two of King Nebuchadnezzar's dreams, which shamed the pagan magicians and wise men of Babylon, who lacked the ability.

Many years after the king's prophetic dreams, when the hand of God wrote a divine message on the wall of King Belshazzar's banquet hall, none of the king's magi and scholars could determine the meaning of the message. Then the queen mother, Nebuchadnezzar's widow, seeing the consternation of her young king, suggested they call for the retired prophet Daniel. "Forasmuch as an excellent spirit, and knowledge, and understanding, interpreting of dreams, and shewing of hard sentences, and dissolving of doubts, were found in the same Daniel, whom the king named Belteshazzar: now let Daniel be called, and he will shew the interpretation" (Daniel 5:12).

THE CHARACTER OF THE GREATEST PROPHET

Second only to Jesus Christ, Daniel displayed the highest spiritual character of any of the fascinating personalities who appear throughout the biblical narrative. Three times the angel Gabriel declared that Daniel received the greatest possible honor from heaven when he declared that Daniel was a man "greatly beloved" of God (see Daniel 9:23; 10:11, 19). Daniel's exemplary character did not waver, despite constant trials and deadly challenges and even great honors that he encountered as he served in the two most powerful empires of his day. Despite his remarkable elevation from being a Jewish slave to serving in the office of prime minister, Daniel never lost his humility, his faith in God's plan, and his reliance on God's mercy.

Daniel reported the events of his extraordinary life without embellishment. Even the astonishing visions and remarkable prophecies that God gave Daniel were recorded in a straightforward fashion. When he was offered the highest honors a monarch could give him, Daniel responded by directing his king to worship the true God and to thank Him. This is an important lesson for each of us today. We live in a spiritually deceptive generation in which Satan attempts to divert the attention of believers to focus on celebrity leaders rather than on Jesus Christ, God's purpose, and His glory. We need to remember that the Word of God declares, "I will not give my glory unto another" (Isaiah 48:11).

Daniel's character is evident in his actions. He and his friends refused to eat the spiritually polluted food that was offered to them (see Daniel 1:8–16). The Babylonians routinely dedicated their food to pagan idols, but God commanded the Israelites to shun such foods (see Exodus 34:15). In addition, Babylonians served animals as food with the blood still in the carcass, which was a violation of the kosher diet laws (see Leviticus 19:26). This unprecedented situation in which millions of Jewish captives were forced to eat polluted food was a tragic fulfillment of the prophecy of Hosea: "they shall eat unclean things in Assyria [a territory included in the Babylonian Empire]" (Hosea 9:3).

However, as a result of their uncompromising stand in rejecting spiritually polluted food, God enabled the four righteous sons of Israel to flourish. They were more physically robust than the other captives, who ate the rich food from the king's table. The Bible stresses the importance of building our spiritual character throughout life so we will be able to stand firm when major challenges come. The writer of the book of Proverbs warns, "If thou faint in the day of adversity, thy strength is small" (24:10). The tremendous adversities that afflicted Daniel and his three friends did not make them strong. Rather, the multiple moral challenges they faced in Babylon revealed the great strength of character they *already possessed* due to their early family experiences, their intensive training in the Word of God, and their lifelong faith in God.

GOD'S DEALINGS WITH ISRAEL

To accurately understand the meaning of the prophecies that God gave Daniel, it's helpful to first gain an overview of the history of Daniel's people, the Israelites. It's instructive to review how God had dealt with His chosen people in the ancient past.

Solomon's son, King Rehoboam, foolishly burdened his people with unjust taxation demands. In 930 BC the ten northern tribes rebelled against Rehoboam, splitting Israel into two kingdoms. The ten northern tribes united to form the kingdom of Israel under King Jeroboam I, while the two remaining tribes, Judah and Benjamin, formed the southern kingdom of Judah under King Rehoboam. Each kingdom was ruled thereafter by a separate line of kings, a few of them righteous but most of them evil. God sent His prophets to Israel and Judah repeatedly to warn the people of His promised judgment for their continued unfaithfulness, but the warnings fell largely on deaf ears. In spite of rare periods of spiritual revival, the prevailing trend in both kingdoms was toward greater apostasy and idolatry.

In 721 BC, the northern kingdom was overrun by the pagan kingdom of Assyria, and the Israelites were exiled to the northern part of Assyria (present-day northern Iraq and Iran). Judah remained a sovereign kingdom for another 115 years. However, God eventually used the Babylonian prince Nebuchadnezzar to bring about His prophesied judgment on the southern kingdom. The people had suffered under a series of unrighteous kings whose evil grew to the point that God finally removed His divine Shechinah presence from the Temple in Jerusalem.

The wicked reign of King Manasseh (697–642 BC) was followed by the brief but equally evil reign of his son Amon (642–640 BC). Amon's wickedness sealed the spiritual destruction of the southern kingdom and the Temple itself. In 2 Kings 21:10–15; 23:26–27, we read that the spiritual rebellion of the Jewish leaders caused God's protection to be removed from the Temple, the city of Jerusalem, and the land that God had given to His people.

One of Judah's most celebrated kings, Josiah (640–609 BC), the son of King Amon, was the last righteous king descended from the House of David. The Scriptures record that Josiah removed the idols throughout the land of Judah. Judah experienced a major spiritual revival under Josiah's leadership, culminating in a glorious Passover celebration in the eighteenth year of his reign (see 2 Chronicles 35:1–19). However, the Bible records the tragic death of Josiah in 609 BC after he disobeyed God.

When the Egyptian pharaoh Necho II knew that Assyria was weakening and no longer posed a military threat, he moved Egypt's armies north into Palestine and Syria. Although Pharaoh Necho warned Josiah against fighting him, the Scriptures record that the Jewish king rejected "the words of Necho from the mouth of God, and came to fight in the valley of Megiddo" (2 Chronicles 35:22). Josiah wore a disguise but was mortally wounded in battle by an arrow.

With the death of its righteous king, Judah declined in power until the nation finally collapsed spiritually and militarily. Three months after Josiah was killed, Necho deposed Josiah's son, King Jehoahaz, and appointed the brother of Jehoahaz, Jehoiakim, to rule Judah (609–598 BC).

As Judah slipped into the final stage of apostasy, the people were confronted with God's promised judgment. Jeremiah had issued God's warning that Judah would be defeated by a pagan nation. "And the LORD hath sent unto you all his servants the prophets, rising early and sending them; but ye have not hearkened, nor inclined your ear to hear. They said, Turn ye again now every one from his evil way, and from the evil of your doings, and dwell in the land that the LORD hath given unto you and to your fathers for ever and ever: and go not after other gods to serve them, and to worship them, and provoke me not to anger with the works of your hands; and I will do you no hurt.... And this whole land shall be a desolation, and an astonishment; and these nations shall serve the king of Babylon seventy years" (Jeremiah 25:4–6, 11).

The Conquest of Judah

With Babylon having replaced Assyria as the dominant empire, Nebuchadnezzar turned his attention to the kingdom of Judah and quickly conquered her. The defeat of Judah began the prophesied Babylonian captivity that was to last for seventy years. In 605 BC, Prince Nebuchadnezzar and his armies attacked the Egyptian forces of Pharaoh Necho II and defeated them at the historic battle of Carchemish. This victory established the Babylonian Empire as the supreme world power.

King Jehoiakim initially accepted his state of subjection to Babylon. However, in 601 BC, Jehoiakim rejected God's command to submit to Babylon and declared that Judah was an independent nation. In 598 BC Nebuchadnezzar crushed the rebellion and deposed Jehoiakim, who was killed and whose body was thrown outside the city walls, fulfilling the prophecy of Jeremiah 22:19. The new king of Judah, Jehoiachin, ruled for only three months before he was deported to Babylon. Nebuchadnezzar's army took ten thousand additional captives, including the prophet Ezekiel, during this second deportation.

In 597 BC, Nebuchadnezzar appointed Jehoiachin's uncle, Zedekiah, to be the new king of Judah under his solemn oath of allegiance to obey his Babylonian masters. Zedekiah eventually led Judah's final rebellion against the king of Babylon, in violation of his oath of allegiance and the specific command of God to submit to Babylon as revealed through the words of the prophet Jeremiah. After a long, bitter siege and famine, the armies of Nebuchadnezzar conquered and burned the city of Jerusalem and the Temple of Solomon on the ninth day of the Jewish month Av, 587 BC.

Only a portion of the vessels from the Temple in Jerusalem were removed and taken to Babylon. Many of the Temple vessels were hidden by the Jewish priests. However, Israel's beautiful Temple, built by King Solomon, was totally destroyed. Describing the glory of Solomon's Temple, Dr. Alfred Edersheim wrote, "But alone and isolated in its grandeur stood the Temple Mount. Terrace upon terrace its courts rose till high above the city, within the enclosure of marble cloisters, cedar-roofed and highly ornamented, the Temple, itself stood out, a mass of snowy marble and gold, glittering in the sunlight."[9]

Virtually the entire remaining population of Judah was removed to Babylon. To ensure that the various captive populations within the Babylonian Empire would not be tempted to rebel against their new masters, Nebuchadnezzar enacted a policy of transferring the populations of various conquered peoples to distant parts of his kingdom. Joseph Stalin would later copy these vast population transfers when he forced the transportation of the newly conquered Estonians from the Baltic region to eastern Siberia in the 1950s. This was designed to break the captive people's patriotism, nationalism, and independent spirit and to integrate them into a homogeneous Soviet Empire.

As a result of Nebuchadnezzar's policy, the entire Jewish population was transferred in three progressive stages to the distant northern province of Babylon (northern Iraq), some six hundred miles to the east of Jerusalem. After the Jews were relocated, Nebuchadnezzar moved a group of people called Samaritans from the area north of Babylon into the area north of Jerusalem (today's West Bank and Galilee). It is generally estimated that more than a million Jews were transferred to Babylon beginning in 606 BC.[10]

The Glory of Babylon

Nebuchadnezzar, a brilliant general, rapidly expanded his new empire until his armies conquered the entire Middle East. He rebuilt and enlarged the old imperial capital of Babylon to become the largest city in the world, with massive new temples and beautiful palaces.[11] He built impressive processional boulevards in honor of his gods Marduk, Assur, and Ishtar. Daniel, Ezekiel, and hundreds of thousands of Jewish captives were marched in chains down these boulevards through the Ishtar Gate. The gate was composed of beautiful blue-glazed clay bricks with magnificent bas-relief sculptures of mythical lionlike creatures and bulls. This historic gate was discovered in the last century and taken to Germany before World War I, where it was rebuilt in the Berlin Museum.

Babylon was strategically located on the most important trade routes in the Middle East, the Tigris and Euphrates rivers, which flowed from Assyria south to the Persian Gulf. Under Nebuchadnezzar, Babylon became the greatest and most populous city in the ancient world, with great high walls and ziggurat towers, gates and temples, and especially its famous Hanging Gardens, one of the Seven Wonders of the World. Nebuchadnezzar fell in love with a beautiful princess from the northern mountain kingdom of Media. When she married him and moved to Babylon, the queen soon became depressed by the enormous expanse of flat land. Overwhelmed with love for his new wife, Nebuchadnezzar built an artificial mountain with terraced hanging gardens in the midst of his capital to provide her with a beautiful mountain view. Early in the last century, German archaeologists discovered the ruins of a group of palaces and fortifications in the northwest corner of the old capital city that may have been the foundations of the Hanging Gardens of Babylon.

The city was divided by the Euphrates, which flowed north to south through the center of the city. The river carried rich alluvial soil from the mountains of present-day Turkey, creating a fertile plain of deep, rich topsoil. The old city on the river's eastern bank had palaces and temples; the new city grew in grandeur on the western bank. The temple of Marduk, in honor of the major Babylonian deity, was built near the river at the center of the capital city. North of the city, engineers built a ziggurat, a seven-storied tower that some scholars believe may have been a type of memorial to the ancient Tower of Babel.

The Greek historian Herodotus (born 484 BC) in his *History* described the city's dimensions as follows: "The four sides of the city were defended by huge double walls, each fourteen miles long. These walls measured fifty-six miles in circumference enclosing a city that contained 196 square miles of land including massive parks and gardens. The defensive walls of Babylon were of truly extraordinary strength. The outer walls stood over thirty stories tall (310 feet) and were wide enough to allow eight chariots to ride abreast on its walls (87 feet wide)."[12]

The builders used baked-clay bricks that were cemented with bitumen, a kind of asphalt that bubbled up through the earth from an immense underground lake of tarlike petroleum that lay underneath Babylon. This substance became as hard as rock once it was exposed to the air. The defensive walls were surrounded by a deep, thirty-foot-wide moat. Once the moat was filled with water diverted from the Euphrates, the defenders of the city could easily attack the soldiers of an invading army with a continuous rain

The city of Babylon, which became the greatest and most populous city in the ancient world

of arrows shot from the high walls. Babylonian sentries could see an army approaching from more than twenty-five miles away from their vantage point on observation towers that stood four hundred feet high. The city was guarded by one hundred massive gates composed of solid brass set in the exterior and interior river walls.

The city of Babylon was divided into sections by fifty major boulevards, each fifteen miles in length and fifty yards wide. Half of the streets ran in a north-south direction, and the other half ran east-west. The streets were lined with magnificent houses, temples, and government buildings. The twenty-five streets running east and west commenced at the twenty-five gates on the city walls and intersected at right angles with the streets running north-south. The city was divided by the fifty boulevards into 676 large squares, creating distinct neighborhoods. The inner squares were used as gardens, farms, and common recreation areas.

As a major trade route, the Euphrates River brought a dazzling amount of merchandise into the city. The wealth of Babylon was staggering, with gold and silver almost as common as materials such as brass. The river was lined on each bank by a very high, thick brick wall similar to the walls surrounding the city. Immense gates of solid brass were placed in these walls at the end of each of the twenty-five major east-west streets. Individuals passing through the gates would walk down several steps to landing places, where they could cross from one side of the city to the other in ferryboats. In the center of Babylon an enormous, thirty-foot-wide bridge, built of huge stones fastened by iron chains, crossed the river. A magnificent palace stood at each end of the bridge.

Many of the key scenes described in the book of Daniel occurred within these two palaces. Babylonian engineers built a tunnel beneath the Euphrates, connecting the palaces. An elaborately engineered system of canals ensured that any excess floodwaters would be diverted away to protect the city from seasonal flooding. During the construction of the canals, to the west of the city they created a huge artificial reservoir, some forty miles square and ten yards deep, to hold the water of the river while they built the interior walls along the riverbanks. Once the walls were finished, the Euphrates was restored to flow on its original course.

DANIEL'S LAST DAYS

The book of Daniel declares that "Daniel continued even unto the first year of king Cyrus" (1:21). Many have wondered if Daniel remained in Babylon following the seventy years of Jewish captivity. While the Bible does not declare where Daniel died, a number of Jewish sages concluded that Daniel took advantage of King Cyrus's decree that allowed the Jews to return to the Promised Land. In the Jewish Midrash commentary, we find a clear reference to the claim that Daniel returned to his beloved Jerusalem when Cyrus declared freedom to all the captive peoples of Nebuchadnezzar's empire (Shir HaShirim Rabbah 5:5).

A fourteenth-century rabbi, Ralbag, concluded that Daniel returned at least once to Jerusalem. Another important Jewish religious authority, Rabbi Isaac Abarbanel (c. AD 1500), wrote that Daniel traveled to Jerusalem following the decree of King Cyrus to assist his Jewish brethren in rebuilding the city and the Temple. However, according to all accepted accounts, Daniel was buried near Babylon in a tomb on the banks of the Tigris River near Shushan. Both the Jews and Muslims in Iraq have protected this tomb for thousands of years.

Chapter 3

The Babylonian King's Prophetic Dream

*Revealing History's Great Empires—and the
Coming Rule of the Antichrist*

But there is a God in heaven that revealeth secrets,
and maketh known to the king Nebuchadnezzar
what shall be in the latter days.

—DANIEL 2:28

IN THE BOOK OF DANIEL, God's prophet is not the only person who receives visions from the Lord. Nebuchadnezzar, the pagan king of Babylon, was given an elaborate dream that described the great world empires that would follow the Babylonian Empire after the king's death.

While the dream was given to Nebuchadnezzar, Daniel was the only person in the royal court who could accurately interpret the dream. And much like the prophecies that God gave directly to Daniel, the king's dream included a remarkable amount of detail. As human history unfolded in the following centuries, the rise and fall of successive empires bore out the accuracy of the prophetic dream.

The King's Dream

King Nebuchadnezzar was greatly disturbed because he was not able to recall the details of his troubling dream. He called for his wise men and magicians and demanded that they tell him what the dream was and what it meant. Of course, they were helpless to reveal the details, let alone the dream's prophetic meaning. The pagan wise men admitted that no one could know and reveal the details of the king's dream "except the gods, whose dwelling is not with flesh" (Daniel 2:11). This angered Nebuchadnezzar so much that he commanded his royal officers "to destroy all the wise men of Babylon" (verse 12).

Fortunately, one of the king's advisors issued a warning to the young Jewish nobles, including Daniel, who were being trained for service in the royal court. When he learned of the threatened destruction of all the wise men of Babylon (including himself and his three friends), Daniel gathered his companions for an earnest prayer meeting. They asked God to reveal to them the details of the king's dream and its prophetic message.

God answered the prayer, and Daniel immediately gave God the credit. "I thank thee, and praise thee, O thou God of my fathers, who hast given me wisdom and might, and hast made known unto me now what we desired of thee: for thou hast now made known unto us the king's matter" (verse 23). Notice that Daniel specified that God had revealed the interpretation to both himself and his three companions. He did not seek to elevate himself above the three other young Jewish nobles. And when Daniel appeared before the king to interpret the dream, Daniel gave the Lord the glory for this supernatural revelation.

Nebuchadnezzar had dreamed of a large statue of a man that was made out of various materials: the head was made of gold; the chest and arms, of silver; the belly and hips, of brass; the legs, of iron; and the feet, of iron and clay. Then the king saw a large boulder smash the statue into pieces so small that the wind blew them away like chaff.

After Daniel told Nebuchadnezzar the details of the dream, he then provided the interpretation. The image's head symbolized the king himself and the Babylonian Empire. The golden head symbolized the enormous wealth and huge military-political power of this first great Gentile empire. The silver chest and arms of the metallic image predicted that the second great empire following Babylon would be even stronger militarily, just as silver is stronger and less malleable than gold. However, the silver empire would be of less value in terms of its wealth and magnificence.

History records that the Medo-Persian Empire, the next great empire after Babylon, raised enormous armies, including the one-million-man army that King Xerxes gathered from more than one hundred provinces of his vast Asian empire. This is the army that he led in a fateful attack on Greece and Europe in 480 BC. The army was so massive that it took an entire day for the national units of the assembled armies to march past Xerxes' throne, which was set on a high hill.[1] Yet this huge Medo-Persian Empire lacked the nobility and cultural impact that the Babylonian Empire had exerted. This second of the great Gentile empires lasted only 207 years and was destroyed by the invasion of the swift-moving Greek armies of Alexander the Great in the battle of Arbela (331 BC).

The third part of the metallic image in Nebuchadnezzar's dream was the abdomen and hips of bronze, which symbolized the third world empire—fulfilled in Alexander the Great and his stunning Greek conquest of the known world. As bronze is of less value than gold or silver, Alexander's empire possessed far less wealth than the earlier Babylonian and Medo-Persian empires. Also, as bronze is much stronger than gold or silver, Alexander's empire was awesome in its military victories.

The fourth and final part of the great metallic image was composed of two iron legs and feet with ten toes that were made partly of clay and partly of iron. Daniel interpreted this to mean that the fourth world empire would be as strong as iron and would trample all other nations with its overwhelming military force. Though it would use its highly trained army to annihilate other nations, it would be of less refinement and value, just as iron has less value than the statue's other metals. Daniel's interpretation was fulfilled when the Roman Empire subdued its enemies and transformed the known world with Roman institutions and laws and a universal language. Much of the world today still uses laws derived from Rome, numerous European languages are based on Latin, and forms of government and armies trace their lineage and traditions back to ancient Rome.

Nebuchadnezzar's dream prophetically described both the ancient Roman Empire and a last-days revival of the Roman Empire, a prophecy that is being fulfilled in our time. The unusual feature of two feet that have ten toes composed "part of iron and part of clay" (Daniel 2:33) draws our attention. Daniel interpreted this to be the final form of a revived Roman Empire that will arise in the last days and will be composed of ten nations (corresponding to the ten toes). These ten nations of Europe and the Mediterranean will include strong (iron) nations and weak (clay) nations, some authoritarian and others democratic. During the time of this ten-nation confederation, a leader will rise who will become the final world dictator in the last days (see Daniel 7:23–25; Revelation 13:1–4).

The great metallic image Nebuchadnezzar dreamed of was suddenly destroyed: "Thou sawest till that a stone was cut out without hands, which smote the image upon his feet that were of iron and clay, and brake them to pieces" (Daniel 2:34). The rest of the statue was also broken to pieces and blown away by the wind. The stone then grew into a mountain and filled the entire earth (verse 35). In his dream, Nebuchadnezzar had seen the Jewish Messiah and His ultimate victory over all world empires. The stone "cut out without hands" is Jesus Christ. Christ will destroy and then replace the predatory Gentile empires with the righteous kingdom of God at the end of this age.

THE FOUR EMPIRES

There are a number of unusual features worth noting in Nebuchadnezzar's dream. First, it is amazing that God identified only four great empires that would rule the known world during the twenty-six hundred years from King Nebuchadnezzar of Babylon to the return of Christ at the end of this age. All four empires appeared in succession during the next five centuries and in the exact order predicted by Daniel. However, since the rise of the ancient Roman Empire in 63 BC until today, more than two thousand years have passed. Despite repeated efforts, no one has succeeded in establishing a fifth world empire to replace the ancient Roman Empire. Charlemagne, Frederick Barbarossa, Genghis Khan, Napoleon, Adolf Hitler, and Joseph Stalin all tried and failed to create a fifth world empire.

Head of Gold: The Babylonian Empire

While the Babylonian Empire is symbolized by the head of gold—and it was, in fact, the most glorious of the four empires—it ruled the world for only seventy years. Nebuchadnezzar died in 562 BC after forty-three years on the throne. Babylon's wealth and military power, which conquered the

Daniel's Description of the World Empires

This is how Daniel interpreted the king's vision (see Daniel 2):

Symbol	Empire	Daniel's Prophetic Description
Head of Gold	Babylon	"Thou art this head of gold."
Chest of Silver	Media-Persia	"After thee shall arise another kingdom inferior to thee."
Belly and Hips of Brass	Greece	"Third kingdom of brass, which shall bear rule over all the earth"
Legs of Iron	Rome	"The fourth kingdom shall be strong as iron: forasmuch as iron breaketh in pieces and subdueth all things…shall it break in pieces and bruise."
Toes of Iron and Clay	Ten Nations of the Roman Empire	"The kingdom shall be divided.… So the kingdom shall be partly strong, and partly broken."
The Stone Cut Without Hands	The Messianic Kingdom	"In the days of these kings shall the God of heaven set up a kingdom, which shall never be destroyed."

known world, was accompanied by great wickedness. After just seven decades, the kingdom of Babylon fell to the dual empire of the Medes and Persians precisely as Jeremiah had foretold. He prophesied that Babylon would remain a sovereign empire for only seventy years because of its cruelty against Israel and its pagan worship. "And it shall come to pass, when seventy years are accomplished, that I will punish the king of Babylon, and that nation, saith the LORD, for their iniquity, and the land of the Chaldeans, and will make it perpetual desolations" (Jeremiah 25:12).

On October 13, 538 BC, the Medo-Persian army, led by King Cyrus, captured the city of Babylon. This was the very night that the fingers appeared and supernaturally wrote "MENE, MENE, TEKEL, UPHARSIN" on the wall of the banquet hall in the palace of King Belshazzar (see Daniel 5). This was God's declaration of Babylon's doom. The Babylonian king and his guests had ignored the enormous Persian armies that were besieging the city. They placed their confidence in the Babylonian army, their virtually inexhaustible food and water resources, and the city's thirty-story-high walls. After the collapse of its army and the capture of the capital, Babylon became a part of the new Medo-Persian Empire.

Chest of Silver: The Medo-Persian Empire

The second world empire, the Medo-Persian Empire, was represented by the chest of silver. It would be stronger than the Babylonian Empire but would be of inferior value. History records that the Medo-Persian Empire raised enormous armies not seen prior to that time.

Cyrus the Great founded the Persian kingdom and ruled it from 549 to 530 BC. After merging his kingdom with the older and smaller kingdom of Media (led by Darius the Mede), Cyrus conquered the Iranians, the

The Kings Who Ruled During Daniel's Career

NEBUCHADNEZZAR (ruled 606–562 BC). The commencement of "the times of the Gentiles" began with his conquest of Judah and Jerusalem in 606 BC (see Luke 21:24; Revelation 16:19).[2] Nebuchadnezzar established the first of the four world empires (see Daniel 2:37–38; 7:4).

EVIL-MERODACH (ruled 562–556 BC). The son of Nebuchadnezzar, Evil-Merodach also ruled as regent during his father's seven years of madness, according to Jewish rabbinical tradition.

KING NABONIDUS (ruled 556–538 BC). Nabonidus was ruling in Tema in Arabia at the time Babylon was conquered by Darius and Cyrus the Great in 538 BC.

BELSHAZZAR (ruled 553–538 BC). He was the eldest son of King Nabonidus and ruled as co-regent with his father. Belshazzar was killed the night Babylon fell, October 13, 538 BC. He had offered the prophet Daniel the highest honor available, "third ruler" in the kingdom (see Daniel 5:16). Some scholars doubted the accuracy of Daniel's book because no source outside the Bible mentioned Belshazzar as a king of Babylon. However, the respected historian Sir Henry Rawlinson discovered at several Babylonian sites, including Mughier, ancient clay cylinders that name Belshazzar as the eldest son of King Nabonidus.[3]

DARIUS THE MEDE (ruled 538–536 BC). Darius, whose name means "restrainer," was the father-in-law of Cyrus the Great of Persia. Following Cyrus's marriage to the daughter of Darius, the Mede joined his northern kingdom of Media to the new Persian Empire of Cyrus the Great, creating the powerful Medo-Persian Empire, which was the second Gentile world empire.

CYRUS THE GREAT (ruled 538–530 BC). Cyrus's rise to power after defeating Babylon created the militarily powerful and very wealthy Medo-Persian Empire. Cyrus was named in a prophecy by Isaiah more than a century and a half before he was born. Isaiah recorded the words of God: "That saith of Cyrus, He is my shepherd, and shall perform all my pleasure: even saying to Jerusalem, Thou shalt be built; and to the temple, Thy foundation shall be laid" (Isaiah 44:28). King Cyrus authorized the return of the Jewish captives to Palestine (see Ezra 1:1–4).

Lydians (Turkey), and the Greek city-states on the Aegean coast. Cyrus then brought his armies to the gates of Babylon in October 538 BC.

Babylon's walls rose more than thirty stories (three hundred feet) high, and huge brass gates by the Euphrates were designed to keep out any potential invader. However, the Medo-Persian forces built dams to divert the Euphrates into a reservoir north of Babylon. With the dams in place, the water level in the river flowing through the city dropped. Cyrus then marched his troops along a dry riverbed into Babylon. The soldiers were able to wrench open the immense brass gates and entered the city near its two palaces. Herodotus described the Medo-Persian victory with these words: "Had the Babylonians been apprised of what Cyrus was about, they would not have allowed the entrance of the Persians.... They would so have caught the enemy as it were in a trap. But, as it was, the Persians came upon them by surprise, and so took the city."[4]

The conquest of Babylon made Cyrus the undisputed ruler of a vast Persian kingdom covering the known world. Cyrus immediately freed the Jewish captives, as the Scriptures prophesied, and allowed them to return to Israel. "Now in the first year of Cyrus king of Persia, that the word of the LORD by the mouth of Jeremiah might be fulfilled, the LORD stirred up the spirit of Cyrus king of Persia, that he made a proclamation throughout all his kingdom, and put it also in writing, saying,...Who is there among you of all his people? his God be with him, and let him go up to Jerusalem, which is in Judah, and build the house of the LORD God of Israel, (he is the God,) which is in Jerusalem" (Ezra 1:1, 3).

Belly and Hips of Bronze: The Greek Empire

The third world empire, Greece, was much stronger and much more aggressive than Media-Persia, just as bronze is a stronger metal than silver. It

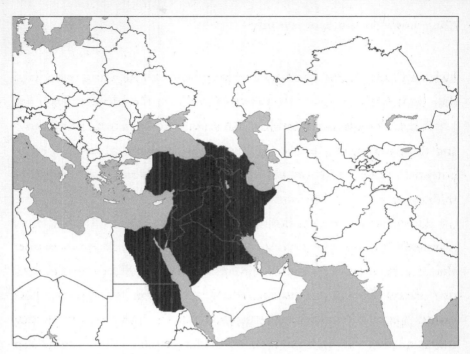

*The Babylonian Empire, stretching from North Africa
across the Middle East to west Asia*

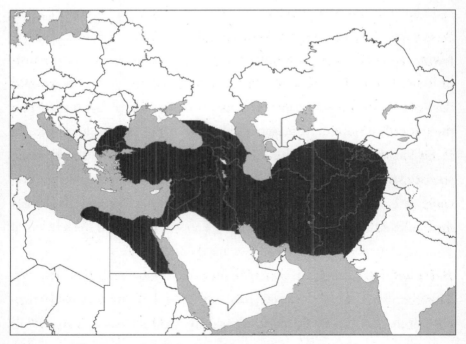

*The ancient Medo-Persian Empire, the second world empire
prophesied by Daniel*

took only a dozen years for the young king Alexander the Great (who ruled 336–323 BC) to conquer the known world from the Mediterranean Sea across thousands of miles to India. Amazingly, he did it with only thirty-two thousand soldiers and five thousand cavalry. Never in history had an army moved so quickly and decisively to destroy far superior numbers of soldiers.

After only 207 years of military dominance, the Medo-Persian Empire was destroyed by the Greeks. At the battle of Arbela in 331 BC, Alexander the Great exacted his revenge on the Persians for King Xerxes' earlier attack on Greece (480 BC). In a vision recorded in Daniel 8:20–21, the prophet described a rapidly moving male goat, representing the Greek Empire, that destroyed the slower two-horned ram, which represented the Medo-Persian Empire. Alexander did, in fact, use revolutionary military tactics, relying on aggressive attacks, highly trained troops, mobile cavalry units, and rapid movement.

Despite Alexander's great organizing abilities, he left no designated successor, and the new Greek Empire was divided after Alexander's premature death in 323 BC. Daniel prophesied that at the peak of Alexander's power "the great horn [of the male goat] was broken; and for it came up four notable ones toward the four winds of heaven" (8:8). When Alexander died in Babylon at age thirty-three, his enormous empire, based on city-states such as Sparta and Athens, was divided among his top four generals, precisely as Daniel had predicted almost three centuries earlier. The Greek Empire in its fourfold division ruled the known world from the borders of India to eastern Europe from 331 BC until 63 BC.

While four kingdoms emerged from Alexander's empire, the two strongest were the kingdoms of Syria and Egypt. The Greek general Seleucus Nicator controlled the large area north of the Promised Land, while

The High Priest Meets Alexander the Great

Alexander conquered the ancient seaport of Tyre in Lebanon in 332 BC. This was prophesied two centuries earlier in Ezekiel 26:3–14. From Tyre, Alexander moved south with the goal of destroying Jerusalem, because the Jewish leaders had resisted his demand for their immediate capitulation. The Jewish historian Flavius Josephus (c. AD 75) described the remarkable events that spared Jerusalem from certain destruction.[5]

As Alexander approached the Holy City, he was met by a delegation of Jewish representatives, including the high priest Jaddua, resplendent in his glorious white Temple robes. Alexander was shocked when the high priest bowed to him and proceeded to tell him that centuries earlier Daniel had foretold his invasion of Asia and his tremendous military success. The high priest told Alexander that God had revealed to Daniel some three hundred years earlier that a great king would arise from Greece to subdue the entire world. When he showed the Greek king the prophecies of Daniel, Alexander was stunned.

The Greek king was so impressed by the supernatural revelation concerning himself and his growing empire that he honored the high priests gesture of submission—and Jerusalem was spared. Alexander then worshiped in the Temple and gave orders that both Jerusalem and Israel were to be treated with great leniency. Alexander also decreed that the Jews should not be subject to the heavy tribute that he exacted from the conquered peoples in the rest of his empire.

General Ptolemy I Soter controlled the agriculturally wealthy Egyptian kingdom to the south. These two kingdoms battled each other for supremacy over the Promised Land during the next two centuries.

Israel finally established its independence through a military rebellion led by Judas Maccabaeus, known as the "Hammer of God." He led a rebellion against the Syrian king Antiochus IV, known as Antiochus Epiphanes, who had attacked the Temple and slaughtered more than forty thousand Jews. Through a series of miraculous military victories, the small underground Jewish forces succeeded in 165 BC in defeating the large Syrian armies after three years of warfare. At that time Israel recovered a measure of its political independence. The descendants of the heroic Maccabees became known as the Hasmonean dynasty. They ruled for a century, until the Roman conquest of Israel in 63 BC.

Legs of Iron: The Roman Empire

The fourth great world empire, Rome, was represented in Nebuchadnezzar's dream by the two legs of iron that broke in pieces all that stood before it. Led by General Pompey the Great, the Roman legions conquered the Jewish kingdom. Pompey arrogantly entered the Holy of Holies in the Temple and installed his Roman garrisons throughout Palestine.

Rome consolidated the nations it conquered into an enormous political and military machine. Rome's awesome military might and its efficient police and judicial system supplanted the former laws and ancient customs of the defeated kingdoms. Even today, after two thousand years, many of our governmental institutions, our bureaucracy, and our judicial codes are based on those of the ancient Romans, and many European languages are based on the Latin of Rome.

The empire was divided into two kingdoms during the reign of

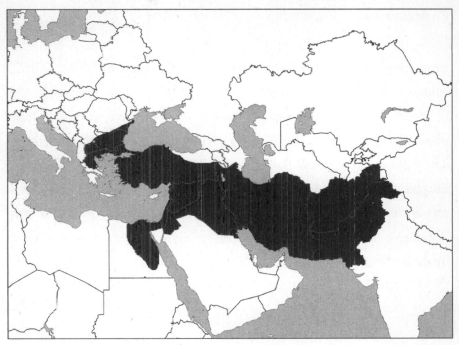

The Greek Empire ruled the known world from the borders of India to eastern Europe from 331 BC to 63 BC.

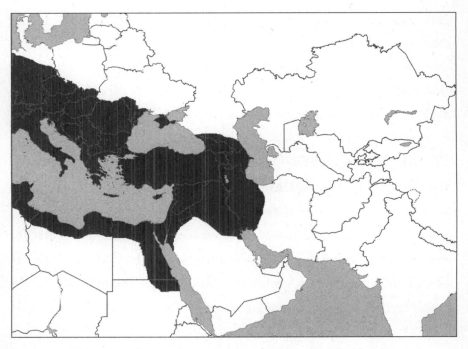

The ancient Roman Empire encompassed much of North Africa, the Middle East, west Asia, and Europe.

Emperor Constantine. The western empire was based in Rome, and the eastern empire set up its capital in Constantinople (now Istanbul in Turkey) in AD 330. The iron kingdom of Rome ruled the known world far longer than any other empire. The Western Roman Empire finally ceased to exist when the Goths defeated Rome in AD 476. However, the Eastern Roman Empire, later known as the Byzantine Empire, ruled a much smaller territory in modern Turkey, Syria, North Africa, Spain, and portions of Italy. Amazingly, it continued for another thousand years until its defeat by the Turks in 1453.

THE REVIVED ROMAN EMPIRE

The last part of King Nebuchadnezzar's dream concerned the final stage of the four world empires, when the fourth empire, Rome, would reappear on the world scene, represented by the ten toes of the manlike metallic image. During the last fifteen hundred years many political and military leaders have tried to revive the glories of the ancient Roman Empire, but failed. Yet God predicted that, in the years immediately preceding the return of Christ, the Roman Empire would be revived.

The European Union—the Revival of Rome

Since the rebirth of the nation of Israel in 1948, we have witnessed the early stages of the formation of the revived Roman Empire. In 1948 the North Atlantic Treaty Organization (NATO) was created to defend Western Europe against the rising threat from the Soviet Union. In 1957 the European Community was founded, with its policies being strengthened by the establishment of the European Union in 1993. This is just the beginning of the outward manifestations of the reunification of Europe. In the near future, the "United States of Europe" will unify to form the revived Roman Empire prophesied thousands of years ago by Daniel.

In its new form, the revived Roman Empire will consist of ten nations based on the European and Mediterranean territory of the ancient empire. Rome will rise again to supreme world power. After it takes form as a ten-nation confederacy, the new empire will first control the nations of Europe and later will take over the world. You and I will live to see the beginnings of this new world empire.

The European Union today is comprised of twenty-seven member states, including several nations from the former Eastern Bloc. Turkey, with its population of seventy million Muslims, is negotiating with the European Union to become a full member. Its well-equipped army (five hundred thousand) is the second largest in NATO, after that of the United States. In addition, the nations of North Africa are negotiating for associate status in the European Union.

The European Union very much resembles the Roman Empire during the days of Christ. It is almost as if God has turned back the hands of time to the spiritual and political situation as it existed two millenniums ago. Then Rome was allied with or had conquered all the territory of Europe and the nations surrounding the Mediterranean Sea. But Rome was never able to conquer the Parthian Empire, which occupied the area of present-day Iraq, Iran, Afghanistan, and Saudi Arabia.

Today's European nations have agreed to create a common European foreign policy and a multinational army for the defense of Europe. The European currency—the euro—is arguably the world's strongest reserve currency, rising in value by more than 50 percent against the U.S. dollar, as of this writing. Since 1978, citizens of the European Union have been able to vote to elect members to the European Parliament, which meets in Strasbourg, France. As you read this, several European nations, including the United Kingdom, have proclaimed their willingness to surrender their sovereign powers to the Executive Commission of the European Union.

THE EMPIRE OF THE ANTICHRIST

Daniel foretold that a future leader of the revived Roman Empire, the Antichrist, will rise out of Europe. He will make a seven-year security treaty or covenant with Israel (see Daniel 9:24–27). Today, for the first time in almost fifteen hundred years, Europe is united and is poised to be able to fulfill this prophecy.

The world stage is set for the arrival of the Antichrist, who almost certainly is now living somewhere in Europe. The prophet tells us that "the people of the prince that shall come shall destroy the city and the sanctuary" (9:26). This prophecy was fulfilled initially when the Roman armies of "Prince" Titus (the son of Emperor Vespasian) burned Jerusalem and destroyed the Temple in AD 70. However, Daniel includes within this prophecy of Jerusalem's destruction a second prophecy that looks ahead to the time of the end—the days we are now entering. This refers to the final attack on the city of Jerusalem by the Antichrist, which will take place at the end of the seven-year treaty that the world dictator will make with Israel (see 9:27).

Daniel confirms that the Antichrist will arise out of the Roman Empire. The "prince that shall come" will come out of "the people" who "shall destroy the city." Since it was Rome and its legions that destroyed Jerusalem in AD 70, it logically follows that once again the "prince that shall come" must come out of the Roman Empire and people. The Antichrist will rule the revived ten-nation Roman confederacy, and he will exercise absolute control through satanic power. Daniel declared that "his power shall be mighty, but not by his own power" (8:24). He will receive from Satan power and authority that will enable him to consolidate his control over politics, economics, and war (see Revelation 13:2).

While I believe the Antichrist is already alive and is preparing to position himself for a phenomenal rise to political power, it's too early to say when this will happen. However, I am convinced it will take place during our lifetime. The remarkable power of new communications technology—including twenty-four-hours-a-day, seven-days-a-week television news coverage, the Internet, YouTube, and social networking Web sites—is likely to facilitate the rapid rise of the Antichrist from obscurity to global acclaim in a very short time. In the realms of entertainment, media, and politics, such a rapid rise to world celebrity status or political standing has been demonstrated by individuals as diverse as Paris Hilton and Barack Obama.

Daniel 8:23–25 tells us that the future king of the world will come forth "in the latter time of their kingdom" and that "when the transgressors are come to the full, a king of fierce countenance, and understanding dark sentences, shall stand up." During a period of evil, the Antichrist will arise. He will be possessed by Satan, filled with satanic power, and deeply involved with occult mysteries. Daniel's words that he "shall prosper, and practise" indicate that the Antichrist will bring about tremendous economic prosperity at least initially. His brilliant economic policies will transform and enhance world wealth as "through his policy also he shall cause craft [the economy] to prosper in his hand."

The Antichrist's success will cause him to "magnify himself in his heart" and will lead to his blaspheming God. Yet the Antichrist will meet his doom when he finally battles the armies of heaven and encounters the Lord Jesus Christ, who will cast him forever into the lake of fire. We will look in greater detail at the events of the last days in chapters 9 and 11.

Chapter 4

God's Servants Face a Test

*Daniel and His Friends Risk Their
Lives in Devotion to God*

He answered and said, Lo, I see four men loose,
walking in the midst of the fire, and they have no hurt;
and the form of the fourth is like the Son of God.

—DANIEL 3:25

D ANIEL'S PROPHECIES TAKE ON ADDED DEPTH and spiritual power when you consider the unusual circumstances under which God gave him these unique visions. As a young man, Daniel and three friends were deported from Judea and sent into exile six hundred miles to the east, in Babylon. Because they possessed superior talent and intellect, these young men were groomed as leaders and special advisors in the royal court even though they were Jewish slaves. Their story is even more remarkable when you take into account the pagan culture that Daniel and his comrades were living in. In order to remain obedient to the Scriptures and the God of Israel, Daniel took a public stand against the king of the most powerful empire in the world. By siding with God's command "Thou shalt have no other gods before me" (Exodus 20:3) and by resisting King Nebuchadnezzar's edicts, Daniel put his life at risk.

While he and his friends had received the best training available in the wisdom, languages, laws, and customs of Babylon, they still held fast to God and His truth. The Lord allowed Daniel and his friends to be taken from their homeland, and God honored them while they lived out their days in a foreign land. But He also tested them—and they passed every test of faith in full reliance on God.

NEBUCHADNEZZAR SEEKS TO BE WORSHIPED

King Nebuchadnezzar wasn't satisfied to rule over the world's most powerful empire. He wanted still more, and the one thing left that would elevate his station in life would be to receive the worship of his subjects as a god. In Daniel 3, we encounter the huge golden statue that Nebuchadnezzar created on the plain of Dura, to the southeast of Babylon. This was most likely the largest statue ever erected up to that time. It was constructed near the city so the largest number of people possible could see the magnificent golden image and participate in public worship of the king. Historical evidence suggests that Nebuchadnezzar constructed the statue approximately twenty-three years after he had received Daniel's interpretation of the dream about the metallic image of a man.

A Jewish tradition holds that the Babylonian king used gold from the treasures taken from Solomon's Temple to cover the surface of the man-shaped statue. It is possible that Nebuchadnezzar chose to use gold stolen from the Temple to emphasize that his empire was built on the ruins of the Jewish Temple of King Solomon, which the Babylonian armies had burned to the ground.

The golden image stood sixty cubits (ninety feet) high and six cubits (nine feet) wide. Naturally, these dimensions remind us of the number 666, which is associated with the Mark of the Beast and his image, which will be the focus of satanic worship during the Tribulation period (see Revelation 13:16–18). Professor George Rawlinson noted in an article in *Smith's Bible Dictionary* that an archaeological explorer named M. Oppert discovered remains of an enormous "pedestal of a colossal statue" in the plain of Dura, southeast of Babylon's ruins.[1]

After the statue was erected, Nebuchadnezzar demanded that he be worshiped. Ambassadors and other representatives from every kingdom within the Babylonian Empire were called to Babylon. Once they arrived, they were instructed to obey the king's summons to worship the colossal golden image. The decree demanded, on pain of death, that every official must "fall down and worship the golden image that Nebuchadnezzar the king hath set up: and whoso falleth not down and worshippeth shall the same hour be cast into the midst of a burning fiery furnace" (Daniel 3:5–6). In ancient times it was common for kings who conquered nations that held diverse beliefs and religious practices to attempt to create political and religious unity by imposing a new national religion. Such a religion usually was based on worship of the emperor as a god.

An important subplot to the larger story of the king's demand to be worshiped involved the jealousy of the king's Babylonian officials against Daniel. At the time Nebuchadnezzar issued his decree, four of his royal advisors were devout Jews who worshiped only the one true God. The fact that Daniel and his three close friends had been promoted to senior advisors to King Nebuchadnezzar aroused the jealousy of several pagan court officials. The Babylonian officials developed a sinister plan to destroy Daniel and his Jewish comrades by suggesting to the king that every government official should worship the golden image. In doing so, the pagan advisors said, the government officials would demonstrate their submission while setting an example for the subjects of the Babylonian Empire, including millions of Jewish captives.

But Daniel's friends knew God's command against idolatry, and they stood firm in their decision to disobey the king's order. "Shadrach, Meshach, and Abednego, answered and said to the king, O Nebuchadnezzar, we are not careful to answer thee in this matter. If it be so, our God whom we serve is able to deliver us from the burning fiery furnace, and he will deliver us out of thine hand, O king. But if not, be it known unto thee, O king, that we will not serve thy gods, nor worship the golden image which thou hast set up" (3:16–18).

In his threat, Nebuchadnezzar had shown his defiance of God. "Who is that God that shall deliver you out of my hands?" (3:15). At first glance, Nebuchadnezzar's contemptuous attitude toward God seems strange in light of the king's earlier acknowledgment of God's power when Daniel was given the revelation of Nebuchadnezzar's dream. At that time the king acknowledged to Daniel, "Your God is a God of gods, and a Lord of kings, and a revealer of secrets, seeing thou couldest reveal this secret" (2:47). However, over time Nebuchadnezzar's respect for the power and glory of Daniel's God diminished.

The probable reason for the change in Nebuchadnezzar's attitude is that during the twenty-three years that followed his prophetic dream of the metallic image, the king had repeatedly invaded the rebellious kingdom of Judah, imprisoned the Jewish king, destroyed Jerusalem, stolen many of the sacred treasures from the Temple, and then burned the Temple. The attitude of many pagan kings was that their military conquests were due to the superiority of their nation's gods over the less-powerful national gods of their adversaries. Thus, it would be natural for Nebuchadnezzar to conclude that his repeated victories over the kingdom of Judah proved that his Babylonian god Marduk (or Merodach) must be superior to the God of the Jews.

THE FAITHFULNESS OF DANIEL'S FRIENDS

After Shadrach, Meshach, and Abednego refused the king's command, Nebuchadnezzar ordered that the furnace temperature be increased seven times. The furnace was so hot that it killed the king's officers who threw the Jewish men into the fire. But when Nebuchadnezzar peered into the flames, he was astonished by what he saw. The three men walked unharmed in the fire and then were joined by a mysterious fourth person. The king declared, "Lo, I see four men loose, walking in the midst of the fire, and they have no hurt; and the form of the fourth is like the Son of God" (3:25). Nebuchadnezzar, a pagan king, saw the Son of God walking in the fire with the three faithful Jews, protecting them from harm. In our own lives, God often does not intervene until we are thrown into the fire of life's hardships. Often God waits before He sends help. He then displays His power to assist us in a circumstance of extreme need. Someone has wisely said, "Man's extremity is God's opportunity."

Some Jewish sages believed that the fourth man walking in the fire was the angel Gabriel who is mentioned several times in the book of Daniel. However, most Christian scholars have concluded that the fourth man is none other than Jesus Christ Himself. Christ came to encourage the three resolute men who were willing to face martyrdom in proclamation of their unshakable faith in the Lord.

An ancient tradition in the Jewish Talmud (Sanhedrin 93a) maintains that the reason Daniel is not mentioned in this story is because he was far from the capital, carrying out government business, when the crisis occurred. Another possible explanation lies in the nature of court politics. In the ancient Near East, it was common for conspirators to launch an initial attack on the less-powerful allies of their enemy. In this case Daniel's three friends were targeted at a time when he was a highly popular and powerful prime minister.

GOD PROTECTS THE JEWS IN THEIR CAPTIVITY

God's deliverance of the three Jewish counselors was so astonishing that Nebuchadnezzar reversed his initial decree and issued a new royal order that provided remarkable governmental protection for the Jews and those who embraced their faith. The king of Babylon now proclaimed, "Blessed be the God of Shadrach, Meshach, and Abednego, who hath sent his angel, and delivered his servants that trusted in him, and have changed the king's word, and yielded their bodies, that they might not serve nor worship any god, except their own God. Therefore I make a decree, That every people, nation, and language, which speak any thing amiss against the God of Shadrach, Meshach, and Abednego, shall be cut in pieces, and their houses shall be made a dunghill: because there is no other God that can deliver after this sort" (Daniel 3:28–29).

The full spiritual and prophetic significance of this new decree is often missed. While Nebuchadnezzar's initial order required only that public officials must worship the golden image, it is certain that the decree would have subsequently been expanded to include all the subjects of his empire. The millions of Jews living in captivity throughout the Babylonian Empire would have been ordered to worship an idol. If God had not intervened, all the Jews who refused to worship a false god would have been executed by fire. By choosing obedience to God, the vast majority of the Jews in Babylon would have fallen victim to genocide.

But God stepped in to protect His people. He used the faithfulness shown by Shadrach, Meshach, and Abednego to miraculously save their lives and later the lives of millions of Jews. It is significant that the famous deliverance of the three Jewish captives was prophetically referred to more than a century before they were born when Isaiah wrote, "When thou walkest through the fire, thou shalt not be burned; neither shall the flame kindle upon thee" (Isaiah 43:2).

DANIEL'S FAITH IS TESTED

Just as Shadrach, Meshach, and Abednego put their lives on the line, so did Daniel stand for his faith in God and against the ruler of Babylon. Years later Daniel was threatened with martyrdom simply for praying daily to God. By the time Daniel faced this personal test of faith, he had risen to become the leader of the council of scholars and royal advisors in Babylon (see Daniel 2:48). Despite his success and loyal service over many decades in the royal court, Daniel had lost favor among government officials in the new regime. Officials serving the conquering empire of Media-Persia hated the prime minister, Daniel, because he was trusted and greatly respected by the new king, Darius. Throughout his life, Daniel adhered to such high moral principles that even his enemies recognized his courage, honesty, wisdom, and spiritual greatness (see 6:22–28).

The events surrounding the crisis of Daniel and the lions' den occurred during the two-year reign of King Darius, the father-in-law of Cyrus the Great. Darius was enthroned as king of Babylon in 538 BC, and he died just two years later at age sixty-four. Cyrus the Great, who married the daughter of Darius, then assumed sole sovereignty over the Medo-Persian Empire, which ruled the known world extending from Egypt, Palestine, and Syria all the way to India.

Daniel had ruled over the affairs of two great empires: Babylon and Media-Persia. He had survived the court intrigues, and his enemies could find nothing to use as an accusation against him (see 6:4). King Darius was so pleased with the counsel that Daniel provided that the Scriptures declare: "It pleased Darius to set over the kingdom an hundred and twenty princes, which should be over the whole kingdom; and over these three presidents; of whom Daniel was first: that the princes might give accounts unto them, and the king should have no damage. Then this Daniel was preferred above the presidents and princes, because an excellent spirit was in him; and the king thought to set him over the whole realm" (6:1–3). Darius was ultimately in control, but he followed the recommendations of his Jewish counselors.

THE PLOT TO DESTROY DANIEL

Ironically, the plot that sought to remove Daniel from power relied on his enemies' confidence in his high character and unwavering spiritual habits. Darius's pagan counselors and wise men conspired to destroy Daniel by suggesting to the king that he issue a new royal decree. The king's order would stipulate that for the next thirty days people in his kingdom should not pray to anyone or to any god except Darius himself. Knowing how much Darius honored Daniel, the pagan advisors falsely told the king that *"all the presidents of the kingdom,* the governors, and the princes, the counsellors, and the captains, have consulted together to establish a royal statute, and to make a firm decree, that whosoever shall ask a petition of any God or man for thirty days, save of thee, O king, he shall be cast into the den of lions" (6:7).

In other words, they implied that Daniel approved of the decree, which, of course, was an outright lie. They knew if they admitted to Darius that Daniel had not been consulted, the king would refuse to sign the irrevocable decree. Clearly, Darius was unaware that the decree was designed to destroy Daniel. Once the decree was issued, the Persian king was trapped by the unchangeable "law of the Medes and Persians" (see 6:8). Darius had unwittingly enacted a law that doomed his wisest and most faithful advisor.

Daniel was aware of the new law, but still he continued his habit of prayerful devotions three times every day to his Lord God. With full knowledge of the conspiracy that was designed to destroy him, he refused to surrender to fear. It would have been relatively easy to disguise his prayerful activities. He could have made it difficult for his enemies to obtain unimpeachable evidence regarding his disobedient prayers to almighty God. However, the biblical account declares: "Now when Daniel knew that the writing was signed, he went into his house; and his windows being open in his chamber toward Jerusalem, he kneeled upon his knees three times a day, and prayed, and gave thanks before his God, as he did aforetime" (6:10). The phrases "toward Jerusalem" and "as he did aforetime" speak volumes about Daniel's utter devotion to God (even in the presence of his enemies). Note that the prophet habitually prayed on his knees. The practice of praying on one's knees is referred to in the Scriptures a number of times, including references to King Solomon (see 1 Kings 8:54) and Ezra, the great leader of the Jewish exiles who returned to Israel to reestablish the Jewish nation (see Ezra 9:5).

Praying toward the Temple in Jerusalem demonstrated Daniel's faithful character and his lifelong love of Israel and the Holy City. Centuries prior to this, King Solomon had referred to this prayerful practice: "Yet if they shall bethink themselves in the land whither they were carried captives, and repent, and make supplication unto thee in the land of them that carried them captives, saying, We have sinned, and have done perversely, we have committed wickedness; and so return unto thee with all their heart, and with all their soul, in the land of their enemies, which led them away captive, and pray unto thee toward their land, which thou gavest unto their fathers, the city which thou hast chosen, and the house which I have built for thy name: then hear thou their prayer and their supplication in heaven thy dwelling place, and maintain their cause" (1 Kings 8:47–49). The prayerful behavior of Daniel and his three friends in Babylon demonstrated their unwavering faith that the Lord had not abandoned His people in their long decades of exile in Babylon. Even today, hundreds of thousands of Jews from around the world come to Jerusalem every year to pray at the Western Wall, the last remaining ruin of the Temple.

GOD'S STAY OF EXECUTION

When the Persian officials discovered that Daniel continued to pray daily to God in defiance of King Darius's decree, they demanded that Daniel be taken to a dungeon where hungry lions awaited their next victim. The king knew there was no legal means by which he could exempt Daniel from punishment, but he did indicate his faith in Daniel's God. "Thy God whom thou servest continually, he will deliver thee" (Daniel 6:16).

The lions had been trained to kill and eat any prisoner who was sent into their den. Daniel knew this, of course, yet he trusted in God's protection. After committing his life to the Lord's care, he entered the dungeon and lay down to sleep among the previously ravenous lions. He trusted that God, who created the magnificent lions, was also able to restrain their natural inclination to attack him. Daniel's survival proved that the angels had supernaturally "stopped the mouths of lions" in response to his unwavering faith (Hebrews 11:33). Ancient monuments discovered in the ruins of Babylon reveal several depictions of prisoners being eaten by lions. An inscription and a stone carving of lions killing prisoners were also discovered near Daniel's tomb at Susa, Iraq.[2]

Over the centuries critics have dismissed this biblical account. The skeptics have argued that the lions must have been fed prior to Daniel's arrival or that they simply were not hungry. However, such theories are proven false when we consider the end of the story. When Darius came to the lions' den the next morning, after a sleepless night spent wondering if God would miraculously save Daniel from the hungry beasts, the king was delighted to discover that Daniel had been delivered. "Then was the king exceedingly glad for him, and commanded that they should take Daniel up out of the den. So Daniel was taken up out of the den, and no manner of hurt was found upon him, because he believed in his God" (Daniel 6:23).

Here is the secret of true confidence, which all Christians can acquire by placing their complete faith in God. "No manner of hurt was found upon him, because he believed in his God." While our bodies may be destroyed, our eternal destiny is in heaven, so we should not fear what man or life's trials can do to us. No injury can afflict us spiritually when we place our lives in God's hands.

When King Darius found out that the pagan counselors and wise men had plotted against Daniel, he ordered that they be thrown into the dungeon, where they were killed by the lions. Obviously, the lions were hungry enough to immediately feast on any available meat.

With the judgment of the initial decree legally fulfilled, Darius issued a new decree that replaced and rectified the royal order pushed forward by Daniel's enemies. "Then king Darius wrote unto all people, nations, and languages, that dwell in all the earth; Peace be multiplied unto you. I make a decree, That in every dominion of my kingdom men tremble and fear before the God of Daniel: for he is the living God, and stedfast for ever, and his kingdom that which shall not be destroyed, and his dominion shall be even unto the end. He delivereth and rescueth, and he worketh signs and wonders in heaven and in earth, who hath delivered Daniel from the power of the lions" (6:25–27).

Chapter 5

Divine Writing on a Palace Wall

*God Reveals the Coming Judgment
to Babylon's Pagan Leaders*

This is the interpretation of the thing:
MENE. God hath numbered thy kingdom,
and finished it.
TEKEL; Thou art weighed in the balances,
and art found wanting.
PERES; Thy kingdom is divided,
and given to the Medes and Persians.

—DANIEL 5:26–28

TIME AND AGAIN GOD WARNED His people about the consequences of their sin and idolatry. He also issued warnings to His enemies in the Gentile empires, pointing out to pagan kings the error of their ways and telling them in advance how He would judge their sin.

God gave King Nebuchadnezzar a prophetic vision of a great tree, which exposed the king's pride and arrogance and revealed God's promised judgment of Nebuchadnezzar in the form of seven years of madness. But that wasn't the only time God warned a leader of Babylon of impending judgment. After Nebuchadnezzar died, his grandson, King Belshazzar, continued in the evil of his father and grandfather. God warned Belshazzar, the last king of Babylon, of immediate judgment by writing mysterious words on the wall of the palace's banquet hall.

The Vision of the Great Tree

No matter whom you compare him to, Nebuchadnezzar was one of the most powerful and most successful leaders in history. Biblical accounts and historical records document his remarkable success in military victories and the administration of government and massive building programs. However, along with his fame and success, Nebuchadnezzar was overcome with pride. He refused to acknowledge that God alone had the power to raise up kings and kingdoms and also to bring them down. God chose to open Nebuchadnezzar's eyes to this truth.

The vision that God gave Nebuchadnezzar is just as relevant today as it was in 569 BC. The vision and its interpretation give us important insight into the rise and fall of great leaders. God alone is the One who raises individuals to great wealth and prominence, and by God's decree many such individuals fall to personal defeat and public disgrace. When a leader's heart is fully committed to God, then the Lord blesses and honors that person's humility. But God opposes the proud (Deuteronomy 8:17–18).

On some level Nebuchadnezzar realized that he owed his success to the blessing of the "God of Daniel." However, his pride took over and convinced him that he was responsible for his own worldly success. He boasted that his abilities and efforts had built the Babylonian Empire, the greatest empire of the ancient world. God gave the arrogant king a prophetic dream to warn him of the coming judgment if he refused to repent.

The Meaning of the King's Dream

Nebuchadnezzar saw in the middle of the earth a great tree that grew to the heavens. The leaves and fruit gave food to all and provided shelter to everyone. Then a holy watcher (an angel) from heaven came down and commanded:

> Hew down the tree, and cut off his branches, shake off his leaves, and scatter his fruit: let the beasts get away from under it, and the fowls from his branches: nevertheless leave the stump of his roots in the earth, even with a band of iron and brass, in the tender grass of the field; and let it be wet with the dew of heaven, and let his portion be with the beasts in the grass of the earth: let his heart be changed from man's, and let a beast's heart be given unto him; and let seven times pass over him. This matter is by the decree of the watchers, and the demand by the word of the holy ones: to the intent that the living may know that the most High ruleth in the kingdom of men, and giveth it to whomsoever he will, and setteth up over it the basest of men. (Daniel 4:14–17)

Nebuchadnezzar related the details of his strange dream to his pagan wise men and counselors. However, none of them could provide an accurate interpretation. Finally Daniel was called. While Daniel was always bold in the cause of God as he revealed divine prophecies, in this instance he also exhibited humility and compassion for the king. Nebuchadnezzar noticed Daniel's hesitation to interpret the dream but encouraged him to proceed. The prophet was distressed because the dream revealed that his king would be afflicted with madness.

Daniel began with these words: "My lord, the dream be to them that hate thee, and the interpretation thereof to thine enemies" (4:19). In other words, the judgment that was foretold would please the king's enemies but not the king.

As Daniel interpreted the vision of the destruction of a great tree, the prophet explained that a terrible madness would soon afflict the king. "This is the interpretation, O king, and this is the decree of the most High, which is come upon my lord the king: that they shall drive thee from men, and thy dwelling shall be with the beasts of the field, and they shall make thee to eat grass as oxen, and they shall wet thee with the dew of heaven, and seven times shall pass over thee, till thou know that the most High ruleth in the kingdom of men, and giveth it to whomsoever he will" (4:24–25). The word "times" indicates a year, meaning that the king's punishment for refusing to acknowledge God's blessings would last seven years.

After interpreting the vision, Daniel urged Nebuchadnezzar to repent of his pride in the hope that God's judgment might be averted. "Wherefore, O king, let my counsel be acceptable unto thee, and break off thy sins by righteousness, and thine iniquities by shewing mercy to the poor; if it may be a lengthening of thy tranquillity" (4:27). But despite Daniel's entreaty, Nebuchadnezzar refused to repent.

Only a year later Nebuchadnezzar was walking in his palace and looked out at the magnificent city of Babylon. The king, forgetting Daniel's warning, took personal credit for the creation of Babylon. "Is not this great Babylon, that I have built for the house of the kingdom by the might of my power, and for the honour of my majesty?" (4:30). The Scriptures report: "While the word was in the king's mouth, there fell a voice from heaven, saying, O king Nebuchadnezzar, to thee it is spoken; The kingdom is departed from thee. And they shall drive thee from men, and thy dwelling shall be with the beasts of the field" (4:31–32). In that moment everything Nebuchadnezzar valued was taken from him. He lost his human reason and his enormous empire. He was reduced to insanity, living as a beast in the gardens of the royal palaces for the next seven years.

There are accounts of a rare medical condition in which a type of insanity causes the victim to imitate the actions of particular animals. Whether this was Nebuchadnezzar's disease or whether God gave him some unique sickness, the king of Babylon lost touch with human reason and was placed under the protection of his palace officials.

During the time of Nebuchadnezzar's madness, someone else would have ruled as regent in the king's place. It could have been Daniel, the prime minister. However, according to rabbinical tradition, Evil-Merodach, Nebuchadnezzar's son, ruled as regent during his father's seven years of madness.

Finally the king recovered his reason. He acknowledged the sovereignty of God and resumed his reign (see 4:34). Nebuchadnezzar's return from madness also was prophesied in the dream: "And whereas they commanded to leave the stump of the tree roots; thy kingdom shall be sure unto thee" (4:26). Nebuchadnezzar ruled Babylon for one final year before his death in 562 BC.

Nebuchadnezzar's pride invited God's judgment. Someday each one of us will render an accounting of how we used the talents and possessions the Lord placed in our hands. And more important, do we acknowledge almighty God for our protection and success, or do we believe our successes are solely the result of our own abilities and efforts? God will hold us accountable for these things.

A billionaire investor or businessperson can be relishing his fame and financial success, and suddenly an economic downturn or other disaster can put an end to the person's wealth, honor, health, or status and influence. Anyone who checks news updates on the Internet is familiar with the enormous number of accusations and legal charges leveled against high-profile business and government leaders. It is easy for individuals in industry, media, and government to be carried away with their pride and then suddenly experience the loss of almost everything.

It is God who has the power to lead men and women to worldly success, wealth, and fame. It is God who rules over human careers and families and even national destinies. The book of Ecclesiastes records God's eternal principle: "Every man also to whom God hath given riches and wealth, and hath given him power to eat thereof, and to take his portion, and to rejoice in his labour; this is the gift of God" (5:19).

BABYLON AFTER NEBUCHADNEZZAR

During his forty-three-year reign, Nebuchadnezzar extended Babylon's control over the entire Middle East. However, despite the empire's immense military power, it lasted only seventy years, as prophesied by Jeremiah (see Jeremiah 25:11–12). After Nebuchadnezzar's death in 562 BC, his empire began to decline. Nabonidus, one of the governors of the empire, rose to become king in 556 BC. After a few years Nabonidus left the capital and moved to the western city of Haran, where Abraham had lived (see Genesis 11:31). Nabonidus left his son Belshazzar to rule as co-regent in his stead in Babylon. This unusual arrangement explains why Belshazzar—the "second ruler" of the empire—was able to name Daniel as "the third ruler" in the kingdom. Belshazzar honored the prophet with this title after Daniel interpreted the mysterious writing on the palace wall (see Daniel 5:29).

The reference in Daniel 5:2 to Nebuchadnezzar as Belshazzar's "father" can be explained by numerous similar instances in both the Bible and Jewish literature where the term *father* was used to refer either to a father or a grandfather. It is important to note that Daniel used the Aramaic language (the Chaldean language of Babylon) to record the passages in chapters 2 through 7 that deal with the four Gentile empires. The Aramaic language has no word for *grandfather,* so the term *father* was used interchangeably to describe either a grandfather or father. In the Bible, King David is described as King Asa's "father" (1 Kings 15:11), even though Asa was born a century after David died. Belshazzar was almost certainly the grandchild of King Nebuchadnezzar.

Many commentators have wondered about the identity of King Belshazzar's father. Virtually all the Jewish and Christian commentators note that the father of Belshazzar must have been the mysterious Babylonian king known as Evil-Merodach, the son of Nebuchadnezzar, who ruled following the death of Nebuchadnezzar in 562 BC. Belshazzar was the last king, the ruler of Babylon at the time of the city's capture by the Medo-Persian army in 538 BC.

GOD'S JUDGMENT WRITTEN ON A WALL

In 538 BC, Babylon, the capital of the Babylonian Empire, was surrounded by the huge Medo-Persian army. While the enemy military forces took up positions to conquer the city, King Belshazzar was throwing a party in a royal palace.

Belshazzar demonstrated his contempt for the Jewish people and his blasphemy against God when he commanded that the sacred worship vessels stolen from Solomon's Temple be brought out from the Babylonian royal treasury. At the banquet, while the Medo-Persian army was preparing its attack, the Babylonian nobles and their wives defiled the sacred Temple vessels by drinking wine from them as part of the night's debauchery. By disparaging the power and holiness of the God of the Jews while praising the pagan "gods of gold, and of silver," Belshazzar set the stage for the dramatic appearance of God's writing on the wall (see Daniel 5:4).

A hand supernaturally appeared and began writing mysterious words on the wall of the banquet hall. When Belshazzar saw this, he called for his astrologers, magicians, wise men, and others who claimed to be able to interpret the future. However, none of them could tell him the meaning of the strange script. The queen mother then suggested that the king call for Daniel to interpret the writing. (The Jewish historian Flavius Josephus described the queen as the king's grandmother.[1]) It is intriguing to note that the queen mother addressed the prophet of God as Daniel, using his Jewish name and not the pagan name Belteshazzar, which had been imposed on him by Nebuchadnezzar. In calling him Daniel, she indicated that the reputation of the great prophet of God was still widely known throughout the empire, especially in the royal court.

Belshazzar was upset by the writing and was desperate when he asked Daniel to interpret the supernatural message. Daniel told the king, "And this is the writing that was written, MENE, MENE, TEKEL, UPHARSIN. This is the interpretation of the thing: MENE; God hath numbered thy kingdom, and finished it. TEKEL; Thou art weighed in the balances, and art found wanting. PERES; Thy kingdom is divided, and given to the Medes and Persians" (5:25–28).

These three Aramaic words have a double sense. The word *mene* is derived from *mena*, meaning "to number," and is repeated to provide emphasis. This word declared that God had now limited or judged the days of the Babylonian Empire. The word *tekel* is derived from *tekal*, "to weigh," and declared that God had evaluated the pagan kingdom and found it to be lacking. The word *peres* means "to divide." The word *upharsin* is the plural form of *peres* and provided increased emphasis. The prophecy written on the wall made it clear that Babylon would be judged, divided, and given to the Media-Persians

In October 538 BC, on the same night that God delivered the written prophecy, the greatest empire in the ancient world ended. Babylon was defeated in the conquest of the capital city by the newly ascendant Medo-Persian Empire, led by King Cyrus of Persia and King Darius the Mede.

THE DEFEAT OF BABYLON

More than a century before Babylon fell, Isaiah prophesied the coming conquest of Babylon:

> Thus saith the LORD to his anointed, to Cyrus, whose right hand
> I have holden, to subdue nations before him; and I will loose the
> loins of kings, to open before him the two leaved gates; and the
> gates shall not be shut; I will go before thee, and make the crooked
> places straight I will break in pieces the gates of brass, and cut in
> sunder the bars of iron: and I will give thee the treasures of dark-
> ness, and hidden riches of secret places, that thou mayest know that
> I, the LORD, which call thee by thy name, am the God of Israel.
> (Isaiah 45:1–3)

Records from the Greek historian Herodotus confirm the basic details of the Persian military conquest of the heavily fortified city of Babylon. Relying on their extensive three-hundred-foot-high walls and the city's seemingly impenetrable gates—in addition to water sources and massive supplies of food—the Babylonians believed their city was impregnable. But King Cyrus formulated a strategy that negated the city's defenses.

Cyrus divided his military forces into three armies. In the final assault, the Medo-Persian army initially approached the city from the north and, after digging a channel toward an enormous existing reservoir, diverted the Euphrates River's flow away from Babylon. Within hours the level of water dropped significantly in the riverbed that ran through the city. This allowed the northern Persian army to enter the city by marching underneath the massive river gates.

Once the first Persian army entered the city from the north by following the riverbed, the second army penetrated the city's southern defenses after taking advantage of the lowered water level in the Euphrates. Under cover of darkness, Persian invaders from the south approached the center of the city, where the huge central bridge connected the two major palaces.

The much-larger third Persian army later followed the route of the second army and entered Babylon from the south underneath the river gates. The soldiers walked silently on the riverbed. This reserve army reached the center of the city at night and took up positions outside the major palaces and centers of government.

Despite Cyrus's brilliant strategy of diverting the Euphrates River to allow his army to breach the city gates, his plan of attack would not have succeeded without the misplaced confidence of the Babylonian army. Babylonian soldiers were so confident in their city's defenses that they minimized the threat of the Persian army while it remained outside the city. In addition, many of the Babylonian troops were drunk from joining in the spirit of the king's wine-fueled banquet. Once the Persian armies joined forces in the center of Babylon, they overran the city's key defenses.

The prophecy that was written on the wall was fulfilled in the same

The Persian conquest of ancient Babylon

night it appeared. Daniel chapter 5 concludes with King Belshazzar's death. He was slain on the night that God wrote out His decree of judgment.

LEADERS OF THE SECOND GREAT EMPIRE

Cyrus the Great, king of Persia, was unique in Bible prophecy in that he was named in Scriptures approximately 175 years before he conquered Babylon. Not only did God identify this king by name, but God's prophets also foretold Cyrus's role as the deliverer of the Jews from the Babylonian captivity and the restorer of Jerusalem and its Temple. Isaiah prophesied, "That saith of Cyrus, He is my shepherd, and shall perform all my pleasure: even saying to Jerusalem, Thou shalt be built; and to the temple, Thy foundation shall be laid" (Isaiah 44:28). Curiously, Isaiah pointed out that at the time of Cyrus's conquest of Babylon, the Persian king did not know about the God of the Jews. Isaiah wrote, "For Jacob my servant's sake, and Israel mine elect, I have even called thee by thy name: I have surnamed thee, *though thou hast not known me*" (45:4).

Cyrus the Great was the military conqueror of Babylon, but he honored his father-in-law, Darius, who was king of Media, by naming Darius as the new governor of Babylon (see Daniel 5:31). (Media was the older part of the newly combined Medo-Persian Empire.) King Darius ruled the city for two years, from the conquest of Babylon in 538 BC until his death in 536 BC. The senior king of Persia, Cambyses, who was the father of Cyrus the Great, died the same year. As a result of the deaths of his father and father-in-law, Cyrus became the undisputed king of the Medo-Persian Empire, the second world empire identified in King Nebuchadnezzar's prophetic dream of the metallic image (see Daniel 2).

The final statement found in the fifth chapter of the book of Daniel specifies that "Darius the Median took the kingdom [of Babylon], being about threescore and two years old" (5:31). But why did the Holy Spirit point out that Darius was sixty-two at the time he "took the kingdom"? Why would God want us to know such a seemingly obscure historical detail?

A number of Jewish sages have calculated the chronologies of the pagan kings, their empires, and the spiritual leaders of the Jews that God raised up to save His people. Several Jewish commentators calculated that Darius was born on the same day, the ninth day of the Jewish month Av, 587 BC, in which Nebuchadnezzar conquered Jerusalem and burned Solomon's Temple.[2]

At the very moment the Babylonian king was destroying God's Temple, the Lord was giving life to Babylon's ultimate enemy, the conquering king of Media.

Chapter 6

Daniel Warns Us About the Antichrist

*The Global Dictator Will Arise
from the Revived Roman Empire*

After this I saw in the night visions, and behold
a fourth beast, dreadful and terrible,
and strong exceedingly; and it had great iron teeth:
it devoured and brake in pieces,
and stamped the residue with the feet of it:
and it was diverse from all the beasts
that were before it; and it had ten horns.
I considered the horns, and, behold, there came up
among them another little horn,
before whom there were three of the first horns
plucked up by the roots: and, behold,
in this horn were eyes like the eyes of man,
and a mouth speaking great things.

—DANIEL 7:7–8

FOLLOWING THE DEATH OF NEBUCHADNEZZAR in 562 BC, Daniel apparently retired at age sixty-six from his duties in the royal court. During this period the prophet received an astonishing vision of four great beasts (or living creatures). The beasts represented the rise and fall of the four great Gentile empires that would dominate the known world for thousands of years. Two of these empires arose after Daniel's death.

Daniel's vision encompassed a span of time that includes the first coming of Christ and the reappearing of the Roman Empire in a ten-nation superstate prior to the Second Coming of Christ. The prophecy of the four beasts parallels the earlier prophetic dream of the metallic image that God gave to King Nebuchadnezzar (see Daniel 2 and chapter 3 of this book).

The vision of the four beasts reveals the same sequence of Gentile empires; however, there is one significant difference. Nebuchadnezzar's dream focused on the military power and outward glory of the Gentile empires during "the times of the Gentiles" (see Luke 21:24). In contrast, Daniel's dream emphasized the greedy and violent character of the four empires. Daniel noted that the four powerful beasts in his vision will arise from the great sea (see Daniel 7:2–3).[1] This image represents the sea of politics and also brings to mind the Mediterranean Sea, which was central to each of the world empires.

In this vision, Daniel sheds light on the political face of the four empires, commenting on the character behind the military conquests of each empire. With that in mind, it is important to note that each of the prophetic symbols depicts a predatory beast.

THE FIRST BEAST: A LION WITH EAGLE'S WINGS

The first beast symbolized the Babylonian Empire. Daniel's vision described Babylon as follows: "The first was like a lion, and had eagle's wings: I beheld till the wings thereof were plucked, and it was lifted up from the earth, and made stand upon the feet as a man, and a man's heart was given to it" (7:4). Daniel's description reminds us of the images of great mythic beasts that combine features from various predators. Such beasts were depicted on the enormous walls of Babylon. It is significant that the Gentile nations of the world have usually chosen images of predatory beasts as their national symbols: Britain, the lion; Greece, the leopard; Russia, the bear; the United States, the eagle; Austria, the double-headed eagle; Italy, the wolf.

This first beast, a lion, had its wings (representing rapid action and military conquest) "plucked." The subsequent history of Babylon under King Nebuchadnezzar bears out the accuracy of Daniel's prophecy. The great kingdom, after having conquered the known world, finally ceased its military conquests, and the king devoted himself to massive building projects. Nebuchadnezzar created some of the greatest monuments and palaces of the ancient world. It is also probable that the plucking of the lion's wings and the beast's being made to "stand upon the feet as a man, and a man's heart was given to it" (7:4) was a direct prophecy of the judgment of God in the seven-year madness of King Nebuchadnezzar.

THE SECOND BEAST: A BEAR

"And behold another beast, a second, like to a bear, and it raised up itself on one side, and it had three ribs in the mouth of it between the teeth of it: and they said thus unto it, Arise, devour much flesh" (7:5). In Daniel's vision the second great Gentile empire—the Medo-Persian Empire—was represented by a bear. This is a fitting symbol. This empire was much like a bear, which is feared as a beast with apparently ponderous movements but, when enraged, is capable of swift, powerful, and brutally aggressive attacks. The Medo-Persian Empire conquered Babylon and virtually every other kingdom that stood before it with its ponderous, bearlike strength. Media-Persia amassed hundreds of thousands of indentured soldiers from the newly conquered nations and continued to crush future enemies.

Daniel's vision reveals that the bear empire was much stronger in one portion of the Medo-Persian kingdom. History reveals that the newer Persian region of the empire was the most aggressive and dominant region.

The Persian kingdom of Cyrus the Great quickly dominated the combined empire following the death of Darius the Mede, and from that point in history the kingdom became known as the Persian Empire.

Daniel's vision of the three ribs in the bear's mouth prophetically represented the Persian Empire's conquest of three kingdoms (Lydia, Babylon, and Egypt). Those kingdoms had formed a defensive triple alliance to stand against the invading Persian armies. While the Persian Empire was more extensive than Babylon in its conquests (with 120 provinces conquered), its government was composed of "presidents and princes" who counseled the king. And surprisingly, the king was required to follow their advice. This represented a major reduction in power for the king, in contrast to the absolute monarchy of the Babylonian Empire.

THE THIRD BEAST: A LEOPARD
WITH FOUR WINGS AND FOUR HEADS

"After this I beheld, and lo another, like a leopard, which had upon the back of it four wings of a fowl; the beast had also four heads; and dominion was given to it" (7:6). This is the third world empire—the Greek empire of Alexander the Great—which in Nebuchadnezzar's dream was identified as the brass belly and hips of the great metallic image (see Daniel 2). Daniel's vision of the four beasts revealed additional details about Alexander's empire.

The small leopard is remarkably fast, extremely violent, and very effective in its attack, which makes it an apt symbol of the awesome military conquests of the small but very aggressive Greek army. Alexander's military included thirty-two thousand soldiers and five thousand cavalry. His army defeated the massive Persian armies numbering up to a quarter of a million soldiers. However, if needed, King Darius could marshal armies from the far-flung regions of his vast empire numbering up to half a million at a time. Despite these overwhelming odds, Alexander rapidly conquered all the ancient Asian empires, stretching from Greece to Babylon and southern Russia (Sythia) and India, thousands of miles to the east.

The prophetic symbol of the four wings of the Greek Empire (see 7:6) foretold its future division, following Alexander's death, into four smaller but still very powerful kingdoms. Alexander's four greatest generals ruled these new kingdoms, since Alexander died without any realistic biological heirs. The four succeeding kingdoms of Alexander's Greek empire ruled the Middle East for almost two and a half centuries until the rise of the Roman Empire, which conquered the known world beginning with General Pompey the Great's conquest of the Middle East, including Israel, in 63 BC.

THE FOURTH BEAST: IRON TEETH AND TEN HORNS

Daniel prophesied, "Behold a fourth beast, dreadful and terrible, and strong exceedingly; and it had great iron teeth: it devoured and brake in pieces, and stamped the residue with the feet of it: and it was diverse from all the beasts that were before it; and it had ten horns" (7:7). The fourth great empire, Rome, would be ruthless in its power. It would devour every nation that resisted it. Daniel's vision that the fourth kingdom has "iron teeth" connects this unique characteristic with the iron legs in Nebuchadnezzar's earlier vision of the metallic image (see Daniel 2). The fourth empire in both Nebuchadnezzar's dream and Daniel's vision is significant because the Antichrist will lead the revived Roman Empire in his rebellion against God and his attempt to destroy the Jewish people.

The Little Horn: The Antichrist

Daniel went on to describe the beast's horns—first ten horns and then "there came up among them another little horn, before whom there were three of the first horns plucked up by the roots: and, behold, in this horn were eyes like the eyes of man, and a mouth speaking great things" (7:8). With these words Daniel alerts us to the arrival of the Antichrist in the last days.

Terrible events will occur at the end of the "times of the Gentiles," which refers to the duration of the domination of the world by Gentile powers. The revived Roman Empire (the kingdom of iron: see Daniel 2:33–35, 40–44; 7:7) will have ten horns (representing ten kings and nations) that will rise within the territory of the ancient Roman Empire (see Revelation 17:12). Daniel's description parallels the ten toes of the metallic image of Nebuchadnezzar's dream in Daniel 2. While Daniel pondered the vision of ten future kings, he saw something new, that a "little horn" (an eleventh king, a man) will rise up among the nations of the original ten kings. The "little horn" (the Antichrist) will subdue three of the ten kings and destroy their political power. The seven surviving kings of the original ten nations will submit to the domination of the "little horn," the earthly leader who will then begin his role as Antichrist and world dictator. He will take over the ten nations of the revived Roman Empire. Then he will expand his empire through wars and false peace treaties until he controls all the nations of the world. He will rule this globe-spanning empire for at least seven years until he is finally destroyed by Jesus Christ at the battle of Armageddon.

The Times of the Gentiles

The Antichrist, as leader of the revived Roman Empire, will play a key role in the conclusion of what the Scriptures refer to as the "times of the Gentiles." This period, spanning more than twenty-five hundred years, began under King Nebuchadnezzar. It was characterized by his demand that all people worship his image or be executed. The golden image of Nebuchadnezzar was a foretaste of the final prophesied "abomination of desolation" (Matthew 24:15; see Daniel 9:26–27), which is still to come. This abomination will be a satanic image or idol of the Antichrist that his partner, the False Prophet, will create during the second half of the seven-year-long Tribulation period, the last three and a half years leading to Armageddon. This period is known as the Great Tribulation. The False Prophet will demand that all adults throughout the world worship the Antichrist and his image—or be killed.

In the gospel of Luke, Jesus prophesied, "And they shall fall by the edge of the sword, and shall be led away captive into all nations: and Jerusalem shall be trodden down of the Gentiles, until the times of the Gentiles be fulfilled" (21:24). The New Testament uses two Greek words that are translated "times." One word is *chronoi,* meaning "times," and refers to duration or length of time. The other word is *kairoi,* meaning "seasons," and denotes seasons of time involving certain events, similar to the English word *epoch.* The phrase used by Jesus, "times of the Gentiles," is translated with the Greek word *kairoi,* indicating the "seasons of the Gentiles." This implies that this period will end upon the completion of certain prophesied events.

In the later years of the times of the Gentiles, the world will witness a revival of pagan idolatry and image worship. A prominent feature of almost every Gentile empire throughout history has been the deification of man, usually in the form of emperor worship. It began with Nebuchadnezzar, then the demand that no one could pray to any god but the Medo-Persian king Darius. Emperor worship continued with the demand that people worship the Greek king Antiochus Epiphanes and finally developed into full-fledged emperor worship under the rule of the Roman caesars. Significantly, a number of modern totalitarian states demonstrate embryonic systems of emperor worship, including North Korea's Kim Jong Il, former Iraqi dictator Saddam Hussein, and the leaders of several Islamic states in central Asia. The failure to reverence an image of the leader can lead to torture or death.

The conclusion of the times of the Gentiles will end the domination of the world by violence and war. Following Christ's defeat of the western armies of the Antichrist and the armies of the kings of the east at the battle of Armageddon, He will descend from heaven to the Mount of Olives to defeat the final attack on Jerusalem by the remnants of the armies of the Antichrist. Jesus Christ will then end the "treading down" of Jerusalem (see Isaiah 22:5), the oppression by Gentiles that the Holy City has endured for more than twenty-five hundred years.

USHERING IN THE KINGDOM OF GOD

Daniel saw what lies ahead in our future, revealing an end-times scene of the judgment of God. The Lord God, "the Ancient of days," will finally cast down the "thrones" representing the last ten Gentile kings of the revived Roman Empire. These kings will be under the complete control of the Antichrist (see Daniel 7:9). The identity of these ten nations will soon be revealed. They will be part of the enlarged European Union, nations that will surrender their sovereignty to join the rising political-economic-military colossus of the new "United States of Europe."

God's final judgment will take place in the presence of the multitude of angels surrounding the throne of heaven. In Daniel's words, "ten thousand times ten thousand stood before him: the judgment was set.... I beheld even till the beast [the Antichrist] was slain, and his body destroyed, and given to the burning flame. As concerning the rest of the beasts, they had their dominion taken away: yet their lives were prolonged for a season and time" (7:10–12).

Some Bible commentators have suggested that this vision of judgment refers to the Great White Throne Judgment or the judgment seat of Christ. However, the scriptural evidence rules out this conclusion. Revelation 20 confirms that the Great White Throne Judgment will involve the individual judgment of all unrepentant sinners and will occur in heaven at the end of the thousand-year Millennium. The New Testament reveals there will be another judgment, known as the judgment seat of Christ, in which God will give eternal rewards to resurrected believers and crowns for their faithful service. This judgment seat of Christ, which is for all faithful believers, will also take place in heaven after the Rapture. (See Romans 14:10; 2 Corinthians 5:10.)

In Daniel's prophecy of the four beasts, he mentions judgments that will be pronounced by the Ancient of days (see 7:1–9). This refers to the future judgment of the Gentile nations for their treatment of the Jewish people throughout history, as well as during the Tribulation period. Jesus foretold that this judgment of the Gentile nations will occur on earth following the battle of Armageddon and Christ's establishment of the kingdom of God on earth (see Matthew 25:31–46).

Daniel's vision continued: "These great beasts, which are four, are four kings, which shall arise out of the earth. But the saints of the most High shall take the kingdom and possess the kingdom for ever, even for ever and ever" (7:17–18). When Christ returns with His heavenly army of angels and resurrected saints, He will destroy both the two-hundred-million-man army of the "kings of the east" and the huge western army of the Antichrist (see Revelation 16:12).

The Reign of Jesus Christ

After describing the rise of the Antichrist, Daniel prophesied the coming of the Messiah and the kingdom of God. "I saw in the night visions, and, behold, one like the Son of man came with the clouds of heaven, and came to the Ancient of days, and they brought him near before him. And there was given him dominion, and glory, and a kingdom, that all people, nations, and languages, should serve him: his dominion is an everlasting dominion, which shall not pass away, and his kingdom that which shall not be destroyed" (7:13–14). This describes the coronation of Christ as King and the establishment of God's eternal kingdom, beginning with the millennial kingdom under the rule of His Son, the Lord Jesus Christ.

The Scriptures assure us that both the resurrected Jewish saints of the Old Testament and the resurrected New Testament Christians will share together in ruling the earth under the Messiah in the soon-coming kingdom of God. "But the saints of the most High shall take the kingdom, and possess the kingdom for ever, even for ever and ever" (7:18). The righteous rule of the resurrected saints over humanity is confirmed in the book of Revelation, where the apostle John prophesied that "they shall be priests of God and of Christ, and shall reign with him a thousand years" (20:6).

Finally, for the first time since the Garden of Eden, humanity will enjoy unequalled prosperity, peace, and justice. The righteous government of Jesus Christ will rule forever from the throne of David in Jerusalem.

Chapter 7

The Vision of the Ram
and the He Goat

*Prophecies of Alexander the Great, Antiochus Epiphanes,
and the Final Antichrist*

For at the time appointed the end shall be.

—DANIEL 8:19

NEAR THE END OF THE SEVENTY-YEAR DOMINANCE of the Babylonian Empire, Daniel received yet another vision. In this prophecy a ram and a "he goat" symbolized the two world empires that would follow Babylon, setting the stage for the first coming of the Messiah, Jesus Christ. Daniel recorded this vision in 538 BC, the year in which Babylon was conquered by the Medo-Persian armies.

In the book of Daniel, the text from the beginning of chapter 8 to the end of the book was composed in the Hebrew language rather than Aramaic. This shift in language signals that these final prophecies are directly concerned with the Jewish people, Jerusalem, and the Temple.

Daniel saw a vision of "a ram which had two horns," with one horn (the second) higher than the other (8:3). This foretold that the Medo-Persian Empire, which would soon defeat the Babylonian Empire, was composed of two kingdoms. Media was the older of the two, and Persia was the younger but by far the stronger and more aggressive. The identifying symbol adopted by the Persian Empire was the ram. Archaeologists have found numerous ancient Persian coins that on one side show a ram lying down and on the other side a ram's head.

In the same vision Daniel saw a "he goat [that] came from the west" that "touched not the ground" and "had a notable horn between his eyes" (8:5). The he goat depicted the future Greek Empire of Alexander the Great, which would rise to defeat the Medo-Persian Empire. Alexander was noted for his aggressive and rapid conquests with a small but extremely disciplined army. The national symbol of ancient Macedonia, the initial kingdom of Alexander's enormous empire, was the goat. Greek coins from the time of Alexander bear the image of a goat. The empire's capital was called Aegae, "the goat city," and the sea between Greece and Turkey is still known by its ancient name, Aegean, which translates as the "goat sea."

Daniel saw in his vision that the goat "was moved with choler [rage] against him [the ram], and smote the ram, and brake his two horns...and stamped upon him" (8:7). This prophecy was fulfilled two hundred years later when Alexander's army annihilated the much larger forces of King Darius III, also known as Codomannus, the last king of Persia, at the battle of Arbela (331 BC). Alexander was known for his rage and his utter disregard for personal safety in the midst of battle. He personally led his army into many battles and sustained numerous wounds fighting on the front lines.

The angel Gabriel appeared to Daniel to explain the vision. Gabriel explained that "the rough goat is the king of Grecia: and the great horn that is between his eyes is the first king. Now that being broken, whereas four

An illustration of an ancient Greek coin bearing the image of a "he goat"

stood up for it, four kingdoms shall stand up out of the nation, but not in his power" (8:21–22). Alexander the Great, though powerful as a conqueror, would be "broken," a prophecy that was fulfilled when the king died after only twelve years of brilliant conquests. The prophecy that "four stood up for it" accurately predicted that Alexander's sole rule would be replaced after his death with a fourfold division of his empire. The phrase "but not in his power" (8:22) foretold that the four independent Greek kingdoms that followed Alexander's rule lacked his military power, ambition, and political genius. While Alexander's top four generals maintained the large territories won by Alexander, they did not continue his conquests.

The four kingdoms (the four horns) into which Alexander's Greek Empire was divided included Macedonia, Syria, Egypt, and Asia Minor. Within a century of the king's death, two of the four successor kingdoms—the kingdoms of Seleucia (Syria) and Ptolemy (Egypt)—rose to a level of overwhelming military and political power over their neighbors. During the following centuries, the northeastern kingdom of Seleucia and the southwestern kingdom of Ptolemy continued to wage war against each other and against the Jewish nation of Israel, whose misfortune was to be the battleground geographically situated between the two great powers.

Daniel Describes an Early Antichrist

The prophecies found in Daniel chapter 8 describe two individuals, one who ruled more than two thousand years ago and the other who will appear in the near future. However, both individuals are antichrists who are deadly enemies of God and His chosen people.

"And out of one of them came forth a little horn, which waxed exceeding great, toward the south, and toward the east, and toward the pleasant land" (8:9). This "little horn" is a symbol of King Antiochus IV, Antiochus Epiphanes, who ruled the Seleucid Empire (Syria) from 175 to 164 BC. He was a descendant of General Seleucus, one of Alexander's top generals.

Daniel's vision revealed that "by him the daily sacrifice was taken away, and the place of his sanctuary was cast down" (8:11), indicating that the daily sacrifice of lambs in the Temple would be discontinued. Starting in 168 BC, Antiochus put an end to sacrifices on the Temple Mount. He persecuted the Jews and profaned their Temple in Jerusalem by setting up a statue of Zeus in it. In 167 BC, the pagan king sacrificed a pig on the sacred altar on the Temple Mount. Sacrificing an unclean animal was a religious defilement and an attack on the Jews and their belief in God. Daniel recorded that "it practised, and prospered" (8:12), indicating that for a time Antiochus IV succeeded in persecuting the Jews as he attempted to create a pagan state religion to unify the disparate peoples and religions of his kingdom.

Daniel then saw two angels ("saints" in the KJV) talking, and one asked the other, "How long shall be the vision concerning the daily sacrifice?" (8:13). The other angelic saint answered, "Unto two thousand and three hundred days; then shall the sanctuary be cleansed" (8:14). Scholars have struggled to find the true meaning of this statement. What is the significance of the duration of the defiling of the daily sacrifice lasting twenty-three hundred days?

Since the context deals with the "little horn's" terrible oppression of Israel, the primary fulfillment of Daniel's vision of twenty-three hundred days must be connected with the evil reign of Antiochus Epiphanes. This time period makes sense if you consider the whole of Antiochus's involvement in Jewish affairs. He first interfered with Jewish worship in 171 BC, when the high priest Onias III was murdered and replaced with a series of illegitimate high priests who offered staggeringly large bribes to Antiochus to acquire their lucrative position.

In 168 BC, Antiochus Epiphanes attempted to invade Egypt. At the time Egypt was the leading producer of grain. The rising Roman Empire sent a delegation of senators to warn the Syrian king that Rome would not allow him to conquer Egypt, which would significantly alter the balance of power in the Mediterranean region. The Roman senator Gaius Popillius Laenas gave Antiochus the senate's demands that Antiochus withdraw from Egypt. Initially, the king wanted to delay his response. But the Roman senator used his staff to silently draw a circle around the Syrian king, the now-famous "line in the sand." He told Antiochus that he must give Rome his answer before leaving the circle. Even though Rome was not yet a world power, Antiochus feared the growing military might of Rome. He angrily consented to withdraw his armies from Egypt.

As an act of vengeance, Antiochus ordered his retreating troops, which were traveling home to Syria through Judea and Jerusalem, to attack Israel. The Syrian army killed forty thousand Jewish men, women, and children. On the twenty-fourth of Chisleu (December), 168 BC, King Antiochus ordered the cessation of the daily morning and evening sacrifices on the Temple Mount, which were offered by the Jewish priests (see Daniel 8:11). By putting a stop to the Temple sacrifices, Antiochus became the first of many "antichrists" who have risen throughout history to persecute the Jews.

An old Jewish priest named Mattathias and his sons, motivated by an unwavering passion for God, led an apparently hopeless rebellion against the Seleucid Greek armies. God intervened, and the small, untrained Jewish army defeated the invading armies from Syria. On the twenty-fourth day of Chisleu (December), 165 BC, the Jewish forces removed the Seleucid army from the Temple Mount and liberated Jerusalem. This victory came three years to the very day after the initial stopping of the daily sacrifice by Antiochus. The next morning, before dawn, Jewish soldiers from the priestly tribe of Levi, under the leadership of Judas Maccabaeus, cleansed the defiled Temple and erected a new, undefiled altar to resume the animal sacrifices.

The Jews searched the Temple Mount and discovered a small vial that had escaped destruction by the Syrian army. It held one day's supply of the holy oil of anointing that was burned in the seven-branched golden candelabra. Miraculously, God allowed this tiny amount of sacred oil to burn during eight days of worship services. This gave the Jews time to prepare a new barrel of sanctified oil of anointing, according to God's command in Exodus 30:23–25. This deliverance of the Temple and Temple Mount from the pagan Greek defiler became known as the Festival of Dedication, or the Festival of Lights—Hanukkah. According to John 10:22, Jesus celebrated this festival. Nearly twenty-two hundred years later, Jews who are scattered around the globe celebrate Hanukkah every year to acknowledge God's deliverance of the Jews from spiritual slavery in 165 BC.[1] King Antiochus's oppression of the Jews, beginning in 171 BC with the murder of the high priest Onias III and continuing until the Temple was cleansed and rededicated, lasted approximately twenty-three hundred days. This coincides with the angelic messenger's time reference in Daniel 8:14.

DANIEL DESCRIBES THE FINAL ANTICHRIST

It is more than probable that the prophecy involving twenty-three hundred days also refers to the events of the last days leading to Christ's return. This is a reasonable interpretation when you consider the angel's announcement in Daniel's vision: "Understand, O son of man: for at the time of the end shall be the vision" (Daniel 8:17). As we approach the final crises of our age—the rise of the Antichrist and the seven-year Tribulation period—and Christ's return, the full meaning of these prophecies will finally be understood. Within the lifetime of the current generation, the visions contained in the book of Daniel and John's Revelation will finally be unsealed and fully understood.

Just as Antiochus Epiphanes put a stop to the Temple sacrifices in 168 BC, the daily sacrifice will once again be stopped at the "time of the end" when the Antichrist, the final world dictator, will enter the Third Temple in Jerusalem. The Antichrist will stop the daily sacrifice and defile the Temple, after which he will be assassinated and then resurrected by the power of Satan. When he comes back to life, the Antichrist's partner, the False Prophet, will declare that the Antichrist is God on earth (Revelation 13:12). During the final three and a half years, the Great Tribulation, the Antichrist will demand that everyone worship him as God, and the Mark of the Beast system—associated with the number 666—will force billions of people to submit.

It is vital to recognize that the "little horn" mentioned in Daniel 7:8 represents a different individual than King Antiochus Epiphanes. The "little horn" will rise to become the future Antichrist to rule the world in the last days. Meanwhile, the "little horn" of Daniel 8:9 arose from one of the four horns (kingdoms) into which the Greek Empire was divided after the death of Alexander the Great. In both Daniel 7 and 8, the individuals represented by "little horns" are motivated by violent hatred for the Jews, and both figures fulfill their desire to profane the Temple in Jerusalem.

THE FULFILLMENT OF BIBLICAL PROPHECY

As we have seen in previous chapters, a large number of Daniel's prophecies have already been fulfilled. Comparing his prophecies with events in history underscores their remarkable accuracy and assures us that he was a genuine prophet of God. A leading example includes the "desolations" that Daniel said would be experienced as a result of God's judgment on Israel's rebellion. Here is a quick review of the prophesied desolations:

1. The seventy-year-long desolation of the land of Israel, described in Daniel 9:2. This occurred from 606 BC to 536 BC. It was foretold by Jeremiah (see Jeremiah 25:11).
2. The desolation of the Temple that lay in ruins during the seventy-year-long Babylonian captivity (587–516 BC), described in Daniel 9:17.
3. The three-year desolation of the sanctuary (the Temple) as fulfilled in 168–165 BC by the defilement of the altar by the Syrian king Antiochus Epiphanes. This violation of the daily sacrifice was predicted in Daniel 8:13–14.

4. The desolation of the sanctuary—the Temple (see Daniel 9:26)—that was fulfilled in the burning of Jerusalem and the Temple by the Roman army in AD 70. This followed the cutting off of the Messiah in AD 32 (see Luke 21:20).

Daniel also referred to three additional desolations. These references predict that the satanic "beast," the Antichrist, will cause desolations in the Third (rebuilt) Temple during the last three and a half years leading up to the battle of Armageddon (see Daniel 8:13; 9:17; 11:31).

Chapter 8

Daniel's Time Line for the "Time of the End"

*The Bible's Detailed Description
of Events at the End of the Age*

And he shall confirm the covenant with many
for one week: and in the midst of the week
he shall cause the sacrifice and the oblation to cease.

—DANIEL 9:27

PERHAPS THE BEST-KNOWN and most widely discussed of Daniel's prophecies is his vision of the seventy weeks. This vision presents the most precise prophetic time line available of the future. In the sixth century BC, Daniel outlined Israel's future, he revealed the exact date of Israel's rejection of Jesus Christ as Messiah, and he described the identifying features of the coming Antichrist.

In his time line of the future, the prophet refers to the passage of time in terms of "weeks," each week symbolizing seven years.

Seventy weeks [490 years] are determined upon thy people and upon
thy holy city, to finish the transgression, and to make an end of sins,
and to make reconciliation for iniquity, and to bring in everlasting

righteousness, and to seal up the vision and prophecy, and to anoint the most Holy. Know therefore and understand, that from the going forth of the commandment to restore and to build Jerusalem unto the Messiah the Prince shall be seven weeks, and threescore and two weeks: the street shall be built again, and the wall, even in troublous times. And after threescore and two weeks shall Messiah be cut off, but not for himself: and the people of the prince that shall come shall destroy the city and the sanctuary; and the end thereof shall be with a flood, and unto the end of the war desolations are determined. And he shall confirm the covenant with many for one week: and in the midst of the week he shall cause the sacrifice and the oblation to cease, and for the overspreading of abominations he shall make it desolate, even until the consummation, and that determined shall be poured upon the desolate. (Daniel 9:24–27)

With these words Daniel foretold both Israel's future rejection of Jesus the Messiah and the final end-times appearance of the Antichrist. The first part of the prophecy—the leadership of Israel rejecting Christ as Messiah—was fulfilled on Palm Sunday AD 32, which led to Jesus' crucifixion only five days later at the Feast of Passover. In addition, Daniel foretold that the future Antichrist would make a treaty with Israel for seven years and then violate the treaty after only three and a half years by stopping the daily sacrifice of sheep on the altar on the Temple Mount.

THE BIBLE'S MOST DETAILED PROPHETIC TIME LINE

In 538 BC Daniel was living in Babylon as he read Jeremiah's prediction of seventy years of Israel's captivity. Daniel knew that this captivity in Babylon

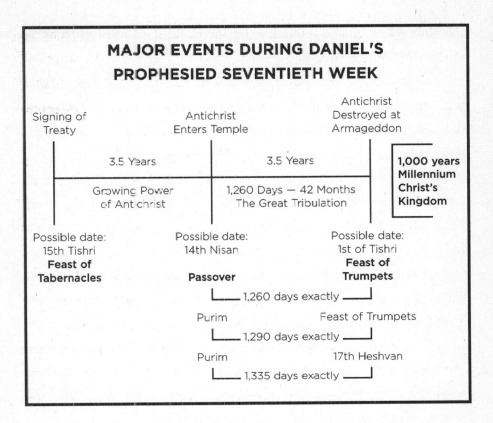

MAJOR EVENTS DURING DANIEL'S PROPHESIED SEVENTIETH WEEK

Signing of Treaty		Antichrist Enters Temple		Antichrist Destroyed at Armageddon	
	3.5 Years		3.5 Years		**1,000 years Millennium Christ's Kingdom**
	Growing Power of Antichrist		1,260 Days — 42 Months The Great Tribulation		
Possible date: 15th Tishri **Feast of Tabernacles**		Possible date: 14th Nisan **Passover**		Possible date: 1st of Tishri **Feast of Trumpets**	

└─ 1,260 days exactly ─┘

Purim .... Feast of Trumpets

└─ 1,290 days exactly ─┘

Purim .... 17th Heshvan

└─ 1,335 days exactly ─┘

(see Jeremiah 25:11) would end in just two years, in 536 BC. "In the first year of his reign I Daniel understood by books the number of the years, whereof the word of the LORD came to Jeremiah the prophet, that he would accomplish seventy years in the desolations of Jerusalem" (Daniel 9:2). Now Daniel asked God for a new revelation of what was to happen to the Jews after the end of the Babylonian captivity.

Daniel's sorrow over Israel's rebellion motivated him to confess to God the sins of his nation (see Daniel 9:4–5, 19). While Daniel was interceding on behalf of the people and the city of Jerusalem, God sent His angel Gabriel to give Daniel "skill and understanding" (9:22) that would enable him to discern the future course of world history. Daniel received one of the most profound and detailed prophetic visions ever given to man: the vision of the seventy weeks.

The Jewish historian Flavius Josephus (c. AD 75) declared that Daniel was one of the greatest of the biblical prophets because he not only predicted future events accurately but he also revealed the precise time when the prophecies would come to pass. The Jewish sages believed that only two of the great men in the Bible—Daniel and Jacob—were given precise information about the mysterious "time of the end." The sages claimed, "There are two men to whom the end was revealed, and afterwards it was hidden from them."[1]

Rabbi Nehumiah, who lived fifty years before the birth of Jesus, concluded on the basis of Daniel's prophecy of the seventy weeks that the arrival of the promised Messiah could not be delayed longer than fifty years.[2] The rabbis taught that a teacher should be at least thirty years of age (Numbers 4:3). Therefore, some scholars concluded that the Messiah would likely be born thirty to forty years before the date that Daniel had prophesied for the "cutting off" of the Messiah.

The Rejection of the Messiah Foretold

According to ancient Jewish tradition, a rabbi or teacher should be at least thirty years old to be accepted as a mature teacher of God's Word. The Jews living in the centuries before and during the ministry of Jesus (AD 29 to 32) understood that Daniel 9:24–26 prophesied that after the "Messiah the Prince" entered His mature ministry (at or beyond the age of thirty), He would be "cut off." That means the Messiah would be rejected and killed at the end of the sixty-nine weeks of years that Daniel described in his prophecy. Therefore, Rabbi Nehumiah concluded that the Messiah would be born approximately 1 BC. At the time Jesus was born, the expectation of the arrival of the Messiah was widespread in Israel based on Daniel's widely known prophecy (see 9:24–27).

This belief among the first-century Jews is borne out by the statements of King Herod's advisors regarding the Messiah's expected birth at that time in Bethlehem (see Daniel 9:24–26; Micah 5:2). Herod's advisors showed no surprise when the Persian magi asked, "Where is he that is born King of the Jews?" (Matthew 2:2). King Herod was so convinced that the prophesied King of the Jews had been born in Bethlehem that he ordered the massacre of children in that small city. Further evidence that the people were expecting a Messiah at that time is supplied by the followers of John the Baptist, when they repeatedly asked him if he was Elijah, the anticipated forerunner of the Messiah. In addition, Jesus' disciples saw Him as the prophesied Messiah, the prophet like Moses (see John 1:45; also Deuteronomy 18:18).

Several Jewish works, including the *Seder Olam Rabbah*, chapter 28, (AD 160) and Ibn Ezra's commentary on Daniel, *Perush HaKatzer* (AD 1150), also interpret Daniel's usage of "seventy weeks" to mean 490 years, a period of seventy sevens (or seventy weeks) of years. The commentary on the prophecy of Daniel 9:24–27 in the modern ArtScroll Tanach series on Daniel points out that the Jewish Talmudic commentary *Mayenei HaYeshuah* declares that "if the Jews had repented during this period [during Daniel's seventy weeks, or 490 years] the Messianic king would have come at its termination."[3] The great Jewish sage Moses Maimonides (AD 1200) agreed with this view, as shown in his commentary on Leviticus 26:16. He wrote, "Had the Jews not sinned again during this period [Daniel's seventy weeks], the complete redemption would have occurred upon its completion."[4] Many of the wisest Jewish sages understood that Daniel predicted that their Messiah was to be revealed in the early part of the first century of this era.

The Biblical Prophetic Year of 360 Days

Many students of prophecy have tried and failed to accurately calculate the span of time indicated in Daniel's seventy weeks. The major reason for this is an often-overlooked factor in the Jewish chronology of Bible prophecy. The length of a biblical prophetic year is 360 days, not the 365.25 days of the Julian calendar's solar year. In biblical times the Jewish year was a lunar-solar year, based on twelve months of 30 days each, producing a 360-day year. The solar year, in contrast, is based on the revolution of the earth around the sun, so it contains an additional 5.25 days. The duration of the earth's orbit around the sun was not known with precision in Old Testament times. According to the article on chronology in the *Encyclopaedia Britannica,* the patriarch Abraham continued to use the 360-day year of his Chaldean (Babylonian) homeland when he migrated to Canaan (Palestine).[5]

The biblical record of Noah and the Flood from Genesis 6 confirms that a year consisting of twelve 30-day months (a 360-day year) was the common measure of time among the early Hebrews, the Sumerians, and the Egyptians, as well as other nations in the ancient Middle East. The Genesis account of the Flood reveals that the five-month interval between the beginning of the Flood (on the seventeenth day of the second month) and the day the ark finally rested on dry land (the seventeenth day of the seventh month) was precisely 150 days (see Genesis 7:11;

8:3–4). This indicates months that consisted of 30 days each, confirming the biblical use of a year of 360 days.

According to the *Encyclopaedia Britannica,* the great scientist and mathematician Sir Isaac Newton, who wrote extensively about biblical chronology, confirmed the length of a year in ancient biblical times as 360 days. He related that "all nations, before the just length of the solar year was known, reckoned months by the course of the moon, and years by the return of winter and summer, spring and autumn; and in making calendars for their festivals, they reckoned thirty days to a lunar month, and twelve lunar months to a year, taking the nearest round numbers, whence came the division of the ecliptic into 360 degrees."[6]

If we want to understand the precise times involved in Israel's ancient history and in the fulfillment of biblical prophecy, we need to calculate prophetic time periods using the lunar year of 360 days. In the book of Revelation, John's vision of the seven-year-long Tribulation period described the last three and a half years of the Tribulation as being exactly 1,260 days (see Revelation 12:6). John also uses this terminology: "a time, and times, and half a time" (12:14). A "time" equals a year of 360 days in ancient Jewish writings, and "forty-two months" of 30 days each equals the same 1,260 days (see Revelation 13:5). These references confirm that the biblical year for both historical and prophetic calculations contained 360 days.

UNDERSTANDING THE VISION OF THE SEVENTY WEEKS

The commencement of the critical prophetic period of Daniel's vision of the seventy weeks was established in the Word of God as "from the going forth of the commandment to restore and to build Jerusalem" and its walls (Daniel 9:25). A careful examination of the Bible reveals that the only official government decree that specifically authorized the rebuilding of the city of Jerusalem and its walls was given by the Persian king Artaxerxes I in the month Nisan (March), as recorded in Nehemiah 2. The decree was dated in "the month of Nisan, in the twentieth year of King Artaxerxes" (445 BC). Using this date as a beginning point, we can determine the date of the final "cutting off" of the Messiah. Sixty-nine "weeks" of years is 483 biblical years. The first sixty-nine weeks of Daniel's vision begins with the decree to rebuild Jerusalem and ends on Palm Sunday, AD 32. This is the date that Jesus entered Jerusalem with His disciples but was rejected by the leadership of Israel.

In 1895 Sir Robert Anderson, a noted biblical scholar and the celebrated head of Scotland Yard, wrote a fascinating analysis of Daniel's prophecy of the seventy weeks. In his book *The Coming Prince,* Anderson proved that the first sixty-nine weeks of years in Daniel's prophecy was fulfilled to the exact day—483 biblical years—after it commenced at the signing of Artaxerxes' decree in the month Nisan, 445 BC. According to the Jewish Talmud (a collection of ancient Jewish religious commentaries, writings, and law), "The 1st day of Nisan is a new year for the computation of the reign of kings and for festivals."[7] In other words, if a precise date is not given—other than the month of Nisan—we are to assume the event occurred on the first day of the month Nisan. The Royal Observatory in

Greenwich, UK, calculated that the first of Nisan in the twentieth year of the reign of King Artaxerxes occurred on March 14, 445 BC.[8]

This means that the time line that is specified in Daniel's prophecy of the seventy weeks begins with a period of sixty-nine weeks of years (483 years), which commenced on March 14, 445 BC. A period of seven prophetic weeks (7 × 7 = 49 years) plus a period of an additional sixty-two weeks (62 × 7 = 434 years), adds up to sixty-nine weeks of years or 483 biblical years (69 × 7 = 483 biblical years). This prophetic period of 483 biblical years contains precisely 173,880 days (483 × 360 days = 173,880 days). According to Daniel's prophecy, at the conclusion of the sixty-nine weeks of years (483 years or 173,880 days), "shall Messiah be cut off." This calculation reveals the date when Israel would reject its Messiah.

A careful calculation reveals that a period of 173,880 days (equivalent to 483 biblical years of 360 days) beginning at Artaxerxes' decree on March 14, 445 BC, ended on Palm Sunday, the tenth day of the Jewish month Nisan, or April 6, AD 32, in fulfillment of Daniel's messianic prophecy. On that day, almost five centuries after Daniel predicted it, Jesus entered Jerusalem and for the first time openly declared Himself to the Jewish leaders and the general population of Israel as their long-awaited Messiah. In calculating the duration in years between any date that occurred before the birth of Jesus—BC (before Christ)—and any date after His birth in AD (anno Domini, "in the year of our Lord"), one year must be omitted from the calculation. There is no year zero. The reason is that the time that elapsed between the Passover in 1 BC and the following year's Passover in AD 1 was only one year (360 days), not two years. (There is no 0 BC or AD 0.)

It is natural for Westerners, who use the decimal system, to divide extended periods of time into decades. However, for the ancient Jews it was natural to group not only weeks of seven days but to group years into "weeks," or heptads, of seven years each. The word *week* could be used by biblical writers such as Daniel to refer to either years or days. Note that Daniel tells us that the angel Gabriel was delayed "three full weeks" by satanic forces in answering Daniel's prayer (see Daniel 10:2–13). In the Hebrew text the prophet clarifies his meaning by specifying that these particular "weeks" refer to weeks of days, not weeks of years (see 10:13).

Israel's Leaders Reject the Messiah

On the tenth day of the month Nisan, April 6, AD 32, Israel's religious and political leadership rejected their promised Messiah. On that day Jesus rode into Jerusalem on the back of a foal (see Zechariah 9:9). The "multitude of the disciples" (His followers) recognized Him as the true Messiah and proclaimed, "Blessed be the King that cometh in the name of the Lord: peace in heaven, and glory in the highest" (Luke 19:37–38). However, the religious and political leaders and most of the people of Jerusalem refused to acknowledge Jesus as their Messiah. When Jesus' disciples openly acknowledged Him as "the King that cometh in the name of the Lord," the Jewish leaders called out to Jesus, "Master, rebuke thy disciples" (19:39). However, Jesus replied, "I tell you that, if these should hold their peace, the stones would immediately cry out" (19:40). Jesus knew that this was the exact day prophesied by Daniel that Israel must accept or reject their long-awaited Messiah (see Daniel 9:24–26). However, Jesus already knew that He would be rejected by Israel's leaders (see Luke 19:44).

Luke described the poignant scene as Jesus approached Jerusalem from Bethany, as they traveled the road around the summit of the Mount of Olives. Jesus was overcome with emotion as He contemplated the terrible destruction of Jerusalem and the Temple that He foresaw would follow their rejection of Him. "He beheld the city, and wept over it, saying, If thou hadst known, even thou, at least in this thy day, the things which belong unto thy peace! but now they are hid from thine eyes. For the days shall come upon thee, that thine enemies shall cast a trench about thee, and compass thee round, and keep thee in on every side, and shall lay thee even with the ground, and thy children within thee; and they shall not leave in thee one stone upon another; because thou knewest not the time of thy visitation" (19:41–44).

Jesus knew that April 6, AD 32 (known to us as Palm Sunday) was a critical day for Israel. Despite the acclaim of a multitude of Jesus' disciples and many of the nation's citizens, the majority of the religious and political leaders rejected the messianic claims of Jesus. Only five days later the people were crying, "Let him be crucified" (Matthew 27:23). The rejection of Jesus resulted in the postponement of the promised kingdom of God for almost two thousand years.

In AD 70, only thirty-eight years after Christ prophesied the destruction of Jerusalem (see Luke 19:41–44), the Roman legions besieged the city, killing more than one million inhabitants. The Roman army leveled Jerusalem and the beautiful Temple, fulfilling Christ's prophecy that "they shall not leave in thee one stone upon another" (Luke 19:44). The fearsome cries of the people, "Let him be crucified" (Matthew 27:23) and "His blood be on us, and on our children" (27:25), were tragically fulfilled. In his book *Wars of the Jews,* Flavius Josephus recorded that during the final siege of Jerusalem in AD 70, the hills surrounding the city were covered with thousands of crosses bearing the bodies of Jewish soldiers and civilians who were crucified by the Romans (up to five hundred every day).[9]

The Final Week: The Coming Tribulation

Jesus was crucified on April 11, AD 32, concluding Daniel's sixty-ninth week of years. At that point God's prophetic clock paused, but only for a time. The final seven-year "week" prophesied in Daniel 9:27 will begin with the Antichrist's signing a seven-year treaty with Israel. The last seven-year week will be characterized by the terror and tyranny of the Antichrist during the Tribulation period. The Antichrist will violate the treaty with Israel after three and a half years. He will stop the daily sacrifice on the Temple Mount, and someone will assassinate him, killing him with a wound to the head (see Revelation 13:3, 14). Satan will then resurrect the Antichrist, and from that point he will be totally possessed by Satan. The totalitarian police control system of the Mark of the Beast—related to the number 666—will be introduced during the last half (three and a half years) of the Tribulation period. The Mark of the Beast will be the enforcement mechanism to assure that humanity worships the satanically resurrected Antichrist as God—or they will be beheaded (see Revelation 13:15; 20:4).

The almost universal interpretation of Daniel's prophecy by both Jewish and Christian biblical scholars assigns the seventieth week to the last seven years during the Tribulation period. Numerous commentaries on the book of Daniel by both the Jewish sages and the church fathers of the first three centuries of the Christian era concluded that the events prophesied by Daniel 9:27 and parallel New Testament passages would be fulfilled in the last days, when the Messiah will appear. It is significant that the church leaders who lived closest to the time of Christ, including the prophet John, interpreted the prophecies of Daniel to indicate that the future Antichrist would arise to rule a revived Roman Empire during the last seven years of this age.

The early Christian writer Irenaeus (AD 120–200) interpreted Daniel's prophecy to teach that the Antichrist will appear at the end of the age and will rule during the seventieth "week" of seven years. Irenaeus declared that the Antichrist's worst tyranny would occur during the last half of Daniel's "week" of seven years, a period of three years and six months.[10] The early Christian writer and teacher Hippolytus (AD 170–235) stated that Daniel "indicates the showing forth of the seven years which shall be in the last times."[11]

The first sixty-nine weeks of years (483 years) focused exclusively on God's dealings with the Jews. After an almost two-thousand-year "gap," the seventieth week will again focus on God's dealings with Israel (see Daniel 9:24). After the Rapture of the church removes all Christians from the earth to heaven, God will focus on His chosen people, Israel, now returned to the Holy Land. They will be a last-days witness to the Gentile nations about the coming Messiah. During the Tribulation period, God will use 144,000 Jews to witness to the world (see Revelation 7) about the coming Messiah and His approaching kingdom, as described in Daniel 11:36–45.

Before His death, Christ promised that "this gospel of the kingdom shall be preached in all the world for a witness unto all nations; and then shall the end come" (Matthew 24:14). The gospel will be preached by the Two Witnesses as well as the 144,000 Jewish witnesses (see Revelation 7) during the Tribulation. The Two Witnesses are prophesied in Revelation 11:3–12, which foretells the unique ministry of the resurrected Elijah and Moses. Malachi echoed this prophecy when he referred to Elijah and Moses in the passage dealing with Elijah's ministry as the forerunner of the promised Messiah (see Malachi 4:4–6). God will protect the Two Witnesses so they can't be killed by the Antichrist until the end of their 1,260-day-ministry, when they announce the coming of the Messiah. Finally God will allow them to be martyrs but will raise them to heaven three and a half days later as the whole world watches. Their witness to humanity will be similar to the message that both John the Baptist and Jesus preached. John preached, "Repent ye: for the kingdom of heaven is at hand. For this is he that was spoken of by the prophet Esaias, saying, The voice of one crying in the wilderness, Prepare ye the way of the Lord, make his paths straight" (Matthew 3:2–3). Jesus taught, "Repent: for the kingdom of heaven is at hand" (Matthew 4:17). Their message was an urgent call for both personal and national repentance in light of God's warning that the day of judgment and the approaching kingdom of heaven were at hand.

When Jesus came to earth the first time, He clarified that "the end is not yet" (Matthew 24:6). The coming brutal persecution of the Jews under the unprecedented tyranny of the Antichrist is called the "time of Jacob's trouble" by Jeremiah: "Alas! for that day is great, so that none is like it: it is even the time of Jacob's trouble; but he shall be saved out of it" (Jeremiah 30:7). Daniel foretold that the final trial of the Jewish people would result in supernatural deliverance of the Jews from the Antichrist when their long-awaited Messiah will appear to defeat their enemies and establish the eternal kingdom of God on earth.

The Tribulation Period

Daniel predicted the main events that will unfold during the final "week" of seven years of the coming Tribulation period. The Scriptures reveal there will be a seven-year "covenant" (security treaty) that will be signed by the leader of the revived Roman Empire, the Antichrist (the "little horn" of Daniel 7:8), with the leaders of Israel and the Jewish people. "And he shall confirm the covenant with many for one week: and in the midst of the week he shall cause the sacrifice and the oblation to cease, and for the overspreading of abominations he shall make it desolate, even until the consummation, and that determined shall be poured upon the desolate" (Daniel 9:27). In the middle of the seven-year period, Jewish Temple worship, including the daily sacrifice, will be violently interrupted by the Antichrist.

This is referred to in Scripture as the "abomination of desolation" (Matthew 24:15; see Daniel 9:27). It refers to the Antichrist's defiling of the Holy Place in the Temple, which will occur after he stops the sacrifice, is assassinated, and is satanically resurrected and will begin the second half (1,260 days) of the Tribulation countdown to the battle of Armageddon. In Matthew 24:15–16, Jesus warned the Jews, "When ye therefore shall see the abomination of desolation, spoken of by Daniel the prophet, stand in the holy place, (whoso readeth, let him understand:) then let them which be in Judaea flee into the mountains."

In relation to determining length of time, the statement in Daniel 7:25 of "a time and times and the dividing of time" is a reference to a period of three and a half years. The Hebrew expression "a time" referred to a period of one biblical-prophetic year of 360 days. The expression "times" refers to a period of two years (720 days). The expression "the dividing of time" refers to half a year (180 days), or six months. Thus the total period of time indicated in Daniel 7:25 is 360 + 720 + 180 days, which equals 1,260 days, or three and a half biblical years. The same prophetic period appears again in the prophecies about the Tribulation recorded in Daniel 12:7 and Revelation 12:14. Daniel's prophecy in Daniel 9:27, "in the midst of the week [the Antichrist] shall cause the sacrifice and the oblation to cease," refers to a point in time halfway through the seven-year period during the prophesied final "week."

Christ confirmed Daniel's prediction that the Antichrist will defile the Third Temple during the last days by committing an act of supreme defiance against God. The Antichrist will spiritually defile the Holy of Holies with an unprecedented act of desecration that will express his satanic contempt for almighty God. The apostle Paul, in his second letter to the Thessalonians, said, "That man of sin be revealed, the son of perdition; who opposeth and exalteth himself above all that is called God, or that is worshipped; so that he as God sitteth in the temple of God, shewing himself that he is God" (2:3–4).

The great Jewish commentator Shlomo ben Yitzchak (AD 1040–1105), popularly known as Rashi, commented on Daniel's prophecy regarding the "transgression of desolation" (see Daniel 8:12–13). Rashi said, "An idol, which is mute as a rock, will replace the daily sacrifice in the Temple."[12] This is a fascinating Jewish interpretation of Daniel's prophecy, especially when we compare it with the prophecy found in the book of Revelation that states the False Prophet will create an idol or statue of the Antichrist and demand that all people must worship the idol or be beheaded (see Revelation 13:15; 20:4).

The Antichrist will launch a brutal persecution against all who refuse to worship him as God. However, at the end of the seventieth week, Jesus Christ will bring His ultimate judgment upon the Antichrist at the battle of Armageddon, and He will also bring in "everlasting righteousness" when He commences His rule of the kingdom of God (see Daniel 9:24).

A Jewish commentary on Daniel noted that "the Holy Ark, the altars and the holy vessels will be revealed through the Messianic king."[13] The sages acknowledged that the ark was not present in the Second Temple and suggested that Daniel's prophecy that the Messiah will "anoint the most Holy" (Daniel 9:24) must refer to the Third Temple, which will be anointed with the holy oil of anointing. The Talmudic sages (Yoma 21b) tell us that "the Second Temple, which was not anointed lacked five things, among them the Shechinah Glory, the evident Presence of the Living God.

But the Third Temple will be anointed."[14] Daniel 9:24 reveals that the conclusion of the seventy weeks will include an event "to anoint the most Holy." This curious prophecy may be explained by the fact that Jesus was never anointed with the oil of anointing in His first coming, so He must be anointed when He returns.[15]

The diagram that follows illustrates the passage of time and the major events specified in Daniel's prophecy regarding the seven-year treaty (the covenant) that the Antichrist will sign with Israel, followed by his breaking of the treaty after three and a half years, ushering in the final half of the Tribulation period and ending with the climactic battle of Armageddon.

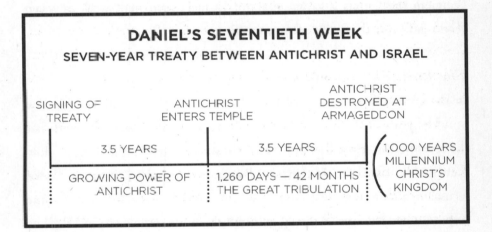

DANIEL'S SEVENTIETH WEEK
SEVEN-YEAR TREATY BETWEEN ANTICHRIST AND ISRAEL

SIGNING OF TREATY — ANTICHRIST ENTERS TEMPLE — ANTICHRIST DESTROYED AT ARMAGEDDON

3.5 YEARS | 3.5 YEARS | 1,000 YEARS MILLENNIUM CHRIST'S KINGDOM

GROWING POWER OF ANTICHRIST | 1,260 DAYS — 42 MONTHS THE GREAT TRIBULATION

EARLY WRITINGS ON DANIEL'S VISION
OF THE SEVENTIETH WEEK

The orthodox Christian interpretation is that Daniel's prophecy of the seventieth week will be fulfilled in the future. Liberal scholars, however, claim that until recently no one saw in Daniel's prophecy the "gap" of time (encompassing the almost-two-thousand-year-long Age of Grace—the

Church Age) between the end of the sixty-ninth week of years and the beginning of the seventieth week of years.

However, the evidence reveals just the opposite. Although the greatest and most profound exploration of Bible prophecy has occurred during the last two centuries, a number of early church commentaries show that early Christian writers understood that Daniel's vision of the seventieth week would be fulfilled during the last seven years of this age. In addition to previously referenced writings of Irenaeus and Hippolytus, numerous other Jewish and Christian scholars concluded that the seventieth week would be fulfilled at the end of this age. Two additional writers, Barnabas and Ephraem the Syrian, also wrote about Daniel's seventieth week of seven years, ending at the battle of Armageddon.

The Epistle of Barnabas

In the commentary Epistle of Barnabas (c. AD 130), written within one hundred years of the resurrection of Christ, we find a clear statement that the seventieth week will be fulfilled only after the Jews return to the Holy Land in the last days. At the time Barnabas wrote this letter, the city of Jerusalem and its Temple lay in ruins. The passage reads, "And it shall come to pass, when the week is being accomplished, the temple of God shall be built gloriously in the name of the Lord."[16] In this passage Barnabas reveals the early Jewish Christian church's understanding that Daniel prophesied that the seventieth "week" would be fulfilled in the future and would involve the rebuilding of the Temple in the last days.

Ephraem the Syrian's Commentary

Ephraem the Syrian was a major theologian in the early church and a writer of poetry and hymns during the fourth century. His works are still used in the Greek Orthodox Church. Several years ago in a rare-book store in London, I discovered a book containing a manuscript from the fourth century (AD 373) that revealed Ephraem's explicit teaching about the pre-Tribulation Rapture.[17]

Ephraem's other book, *The Cave of Treasures,* written in AD 370, includes a section on the genealogy of Jesus Christ. Ephraem taught that the sixty-ninth week of Daniel's vision concluded with the "cutting off" (see Daniel 9:24–27), the rejection and crucifixion of Jesus. He wrote, "The Jews have no longer among them a king, or a priest, or a prophet, or a Passover, even as Daniel prophesied concerning them, saying, 'After two and sixty weeks Christ shall be slain, and the city of holiness shall be laid waste until the completion of things decreed' (Daniel 9:26). That is to say, for ever and ever."[18]

However, in a later section of Ephraem's book dealing with the War of Gog and Magog (see Ezekiel 38:2), he wrote about the remaining (seventieth) week of Daniel as follows: "At the end of the world and at the final consummation.. suddenly the gates of the north shall be opened.... They will destroy the earth, and there will be none able to stand before them. After one week [seven years] of that sore affliction [the Tribulation], they will all be destroyed in the plain of Joppa.... Then will the son of perdition appear, of the seed and of the tribe of Dan.... He will go into Jerusalem and will sit upon a throne in the Temple saying, 'I am the Christ,' and he will be borne aloft by legions of devils like a king and a lawgiver, naming himself god.... The time of the error of the Anti-Christ will last two years and a half, but others say three-years-and-six months."[19]

This confirms that certain Bible commentators from as early as the second century to the fourth century of the Christian era understood that the events predicted in the final "week" of Daniel's vision of the seventieth week would be fulfilled only when the future Antichrist will arise to rule the Roman Empire and defile the rebuilt Temple at the end of this age. Although there are puzzling elements in Ephraem's interpretation of the events of the last days, it is clear that he and other early Christians understood more than sixteen hundred years ago that the last "week" of Daniel's vision will be fulfilled in the final days of this age.

The "Gap" in the Seventy Weeks Explained

Jesus prophesied the final judgment that was coming to Israel in the days following their leaders' rejection of Him as their Messiah: "If thou hadst known, even thou, at least in this thy day, the things which belong unto thy peace! but now they are hid from thine eyes. For the days shall come upon thee,...and they shall not leave in thee one stone upon another; because thou knewest not the time of thy visitation" (Luke 19:42–44). Following is a diagram that illustrates the passage of time and the major events specified in Daniel's vision of the seventy weeks, including the almost-two-thousand-year gap, or "parenthesis," the Age of Grace, during which the church has been bearing witness of Christ.

A parallel to the "gap," the postponement of the promised kingdom of Christ, is found in the Old Testament when the children of Israel halted at the edge of the Promised Land just months after escaping slavery in Egypt. They waited for the reports of the twelve tribal leaders whom Moses sent to spy out the land of Canaan. If the people of Israel and the twelve spies had trusted and obeyed God, who had just delivered them from centuries of bondage in Egypt, they could have immediately entered and possessed the Promised Land.

The twelve spies returned to give their report, and ten of the spies claimed it was impossible for the Hebrews to defeat the people who occu-

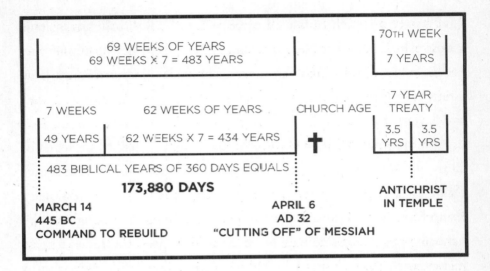

pied the land. However, two of the spies, Joshua and Caleb, said God would give them the victory, allowing the Jews to claim the Promised Land. The people tragically rejected God's word and His chosen leader, Moses (see Numbers 14:1–10). The rejection of God's command led to the Jews' enduring forty years in the Sinai wilderness. That entire generation was lost, with the exception of Joshua and Caleb, the two faithful spies. The remainder of the people who were twenty years old or older when they left Egypt never saw the Hebrews possess the land of Canaan (see Deuteronomy 1:35–38). The entry into the Promised Land was postponed for forty years until a new generation of Jews had grown up in the wilderness and was ready to believe and to inherit God's promises to Israel.

In a similar manner, the leaders of the nation of Israel failed to recognize its prophesied Messiah in AD 32. As a result, the Jewish people have waited almost two thousand years to return to the Promised Land. They finally returned to create the nation of Israel on May 15, 1948.

During this long interval between the end of the sixty-ninth week (AD 32) and the future beginning of the seventieth week of seven years,

God created a church composed of Gentile and Jewish believers in Jesus Christ. The church has been proclaiming the gospel of Christ and witnessing to the world, offering the message of God's salvation through Jesus Christ to any who will repent of their sins and accept Him as their Lord and Savior.

Jesus promised that "this gospel of the kingdom shall be preached in all the world for a witness unto all nations; and then shall the end come" (Matthew 24:14). Through tremendous sacrifice and efforts of missionary evangelism in the last 160 years, hundreds of millions throughout the nations of the third world have heard the gospel. The latest studies suggest that every single day up to 125,000 people are now placing their trust in Jesus Christ. Christianity, with more than 2.3 billion adherents, is the largest religion in the world and is growing twice as fast as Islam.[20]

By evangelizing the world in preparation for the "time of the end," the church has accomplished what God called it to do. The seventieth "week" of Daniel's vision reveals the final seven years of this age and will be fulfilled in our generation. After a majority of the religious and political leaders of Israel rejected the Messiah in the first century, God postponed the establishment of the Messiah's kingdom for almost two thousand years. But the Messiah, Jesus Christ, will soon return to defeat Satan and to establish His perfect rule on earth.

Chapter 9

An Angel Reveals the Future

What Lies Ahead for Our Generation?

Now I am come to make thee understand
what shall befall thy people
in the latter days: for yet the vision
is for many days.

—THE ANGEL GABRIEL IN DANIEL 10:14

I N THE FINAL SIX CHAPTERS OF THE BOOK OF DANIEL, the prophet describes in detail the actions of the Antichrist during the Tribulation period. Daniel reveals the chronology of the Tribulation, starting with the Antichrist signing a treaty with Israel. He identifies the midpoint event that will greatly intensify the coming persecution of the Jews and reveals the timing of the assassination and satanic resurrection of the Antichrist. According to Daniel and other prophets, these things will almost certainly take place in our generation, the generation that witnessed the fulfillment of the prophecy of the rebirth of Israel in 1948.[1]

In the latter part of the book of Daniel, the angel Gabriel appears to interpret the meaning of certain of Daniel's visions (see Daniel 10:14). In the third year of King Cyrus's rule over Babylon, Daniel was praying and "mourning" in his concern for the ultimate future of the Jews (10:1–2). This occurred some years after Daniel's vision of the ram and the he goat (see Daniel 8 and chapter 7 of this book). As he was praying, he received a new vision: "Behold a certain man clothed in linen, whose loins were girded with fine gold of Uphaz: his body also was like the beryl, and his face as the appearance of lightning, and his eyes as lamps of fire, and his arms and his feet like in colour to polished brass, and the voice of his words like the voice of a multitude" (Daniel 10:5–6).

The "certain man" of the vision was the Son of God, Jesus Christ. Compare Daniel's description with the vision recorded by the apostle John: "And in the midst of the seven candlesticks one like unto the Son of man, clothed with a garment down to the foot, and girt about the paps with a golden girdle. His head and his hairs were white like wool, as white as snow; and his eyes were as a flame of fire; and his feet like unto fine brass, as if they burned in a furnace; and his voice as the sound of many waters" (Revelation 1:13–15). After Daniel saw the vision of the Son of God, an angel appeared to explain its meaning.

THE ANGEL AND THE DEMONIC AGENTS

The angel Gabriel explained, "I am come to make thee understand what shall befall thy people in the latter days: for yet the vision is for many days" (Daniel 10:14). He also explained that before he came from heaven to visit Daniel, he was delayed for a period of three weeks. He told Daniel, "I am come for thy words. But the prince of the kingdom of Persia withstood me one and twenty days: but, lo, Michael, one of the chief princes, came to help me; and I remained there with the kings of Persia" (10:12–13). The archangel Michael helped Gabriel defeat Satan's demonic agents that had attempted to prevent Gabriel from answering Daniel's prayer for guidance. We are told in the book of Jude that Michael, the only archangel mentioned in the Scriptures, stands in a special protector relationship to the nation of Israel. "Yet Michael the archangel, when contending with the devil he disputed about the body of Moses, durst not bring against him a railing accusation, but said, The Lord rebuke thee" (Jude 9).

This curious passage in Daniel 10:14–20 introduces a fascinating but little-understood aspect of the invisible spiritual world we inhabit. Gabriel revealed that "the prince of the kingdom of Persia" (10:13) and the "prince of Grecia" (10:20) were demonic agents of Satan's fallen angels who rebelled against God and joined with Satan in the dateless past. They were assigned to each of the earth's kingdoms in active spiritual opposition to the messenger angel Gabriel, whom God sent to advise Daniel. This allusion to continuous spiritual warfare is confirmed in the book of Ephesians. The apostle Paul referred to Satan as "the prince of the power of the air" (2:2). Later, Paul described the spiritual warfare we may encounter: "For we wrestle not against flesh and blood, but against principalities, against powers, against the rulers of the darkness of this world, against spiritual wickedness in high places" (6:12).

Throughout the Scriptures we find that the names of God's angels are revealed. Rabbi Moses Maimonides (AD 1200), who codified all major Jewish religious law in his fourteen-volume *Mishneh Torah,* noted in his commentary on Genesis that the Hebrew name of every angel identified in Scripture ends with the suffix *-el,* which signifies "God."[2] Examples include Gabriel, whose name in Hebrew means "the angel of strength," and the archangel Michael, whose name means "who is like God?"

The Bible affirms that Christ's final victory over Satan will involve violent spiritual warfare in heaven that will parallel the physical violence between the armies of the east and west that will occur on earth. John prophesied, "And there was war in heaven: Michael and his angels fought against the dragon; and the dragon fought and his angels, and prevailed not; neither was their place found any more in heaven. And the great dragon was cast out, that old serpent, called the Devil, and Satan, which deceiveth the whole world: he was cast out into the earth, and his angels were cast out with him" (Revelation 12:7–9). When Satan and his fallen angels are cast down to earth, they will persecute the Jews (Israel—"the woman") and "make war with the remnant of her seed" (the Jews who as Tribulation saints accept Jesus as Messiah during the Tribulation) (Revelation 12:13, 17).

THE PROPHECY ABOUT ANTIOCHUS EPIPHANES

In the eleventh chapter of the book of Daniel, the prophet speaks about the king of the future Greek Empire as well as the conflict between the two major successor kingdoms of the Greek Empire—the Syrian and Egyptian kingdoms (verses 5–20). The reference in verse 3 to the "mighty king" refers to Alexander the Great, who conquered the Persian Empire and the whole of the known world in only a dozen years. Alexander died prematurely in 323 BC in Babylon. Following Alexander's death, his empire was divided among his four leading generals.

Cassander was to rule Macedonia, the home kingdom in Greece; Lysimachus was appointed to rule Thrace and Asia Minor; Ptolemy I was to rule Egypt (the Ptolemaic dynasty ruled Egypt for three centuries from 323 to 30 BC); and Seleucus I was to rule the kingdom of Syria and the major portion of the Near East. His successors, known as the Seleucids, ruled Syria for two and a half centuries, until the rise of Rome. The Roman

Alexander the Great, king of the ancient Greek Empire

general Pompey the Great conquered the Middle East, including Israel, in 63 BC. That victory launched the fourth Gentile world empire of Daniel's prophecy, the Roman Empire (see Daniel 2 and 7).

The complex and rather convoluted history of the conflict between the two major successor kingdoms of Alexander's Greek Empire, Syria and Egypt, is prophetically described in Daniel 11:3–27. Daniel prophesied the unusual and deadly career of the future king of Syria, Antiochus IV (Antiochus Epiphanes), who was symbolized in Daniel's prophecies as the "little horn" (Daniel 8:23–25). Daniel also predicted the defiling of the Jewish Temple by Antiochus Epiphanes that lasted for precisely three years, from 168 to 165 BC.

The same Syrian king is the focus of Daniel's vision in Daniel 11:36. However, in verses 36–45, the prophet looks forward in time to the last days and reveals the final Antichrist, the willful king, and his satanic activities during the Tribulation period and ending with his death at the battle of Armageddon.

THE ANGEL DESCRIBES OUR GENERATION

In the last chapter of the book of Daniel, the angel revealed remarkable details about the conditions that will prevail in the world at "the time of the end." In these descriptions, Gabriel prophesied about the generation that you and I live in. Of particular interest is the revelation about the Great Tribulation, which comes during the last half of Daniel's seventieth week of years. There will be no guesswork about the day when the Tribulation period begins. When a seven-year treaty is signed between the world dictator (the Antichrist) and the nation of Israel, those who have studied Daniel's prophecies will know the Tribulation period has begun.

The seven-year treaty, or "covenant" (see Daniel 9:27), signed by the Antichrist and Israel will start the clock ticking in a seven-year-long countdown moving inexorably to the battle of Armageddon. The seven-biblical-year countdown (7 x 360 days per year = 2,520 days) will continue from the signing of the Antichrist's treaty to the conclusion of the final battle of Armageddon. Jesus Christ will descend to earth to save His chosen people by destroying the armies clashing in northern Israel (see Daniel 12:1; Revelation 19:11, 14, 19–20). During the Tribulation period, following the Rapture of all Christians to heaven (see 1 Thessalonians 1:10; 4:16–17), the Bible warns that the wrath of God will be poured out on unrepentant sinners. These wrath judgments described in Revelation 6:1–17 include worldwide war, famine, plague, wild animals attacking humans, and massive global earthquakes. These terrible judgments commence at the beginning of the seven-year Tribulation period after the treaty is signed by the Antichrist. They will continue and be joined by the additional judgments prophesied by the prophet John (Revelation 6–18).

However, the second half of the seven-year Tribulation period will be even worse. The last three and a half years will begin with the Antichrist's violation of the treaty with Israel. He will break the covenant by stopping the sacrifice and defiling the Holy of Holies in the rebuilt Temple in Jerusalem. This prophesied "abomination of desolation" (see Daniel 9:26–27; Matthew 24:15) will signal the beginning of the final 1,260 days (three and a half years) until the seven-year Tribulation period ends at the conclusion of the battle of Armageddon with Christ's victory.

The Tribulation will be a time of such unprecedented suffering that God sent His prophets to prepare His people with knowledge of what is to come. The Lord gave believers the assurance that He will preserve and save them through the Rapture (resurrection to heaven) to join His Son, Jesus

Christ. Those without a spiritual understanding of the Bible or personal faith in Christ will find Daniel's prophecies incomprehensible. They will miss out on understanding both the warnings of the last days and the hope of heaven that God provides. However, Daniel promises that Christians who are "wise shall understand" (Daniel 12:10).

The prophecies concerning the Tribulation in the books of Daniel and Revelation indicate the Tribulation will last seven years of 360 days, or a total of 2,520 days. It is probable that God provided this timetable to encourage the new "Tribulation saints"—those who become believers in the Messiah after the Rapture during this time of persecution—to persevere. He wanted to give the Tribulation saints hope in the knowledge that the returning Messiah will defeat the Antichrist and his armies at the end of the Tribulation. It will appear to be impossible to escape the forces of the Antichrist, but God has given the Tribulation saints this timetable to encourage them to resist Satan because God has declared the day in which the Antichrist will be defeated.

A period of time lasting 1,290 days will begin with the Antichrist's stopping the daily sacrifice in the rebuilt Temple. The prophecies of both Daniel and John, in Revelation, foretell that the last three and a half years (1,260 days) of the seven-year Tribulation will end at the battle of Armageddon. However, Daniel also revealed that a period of 1,290 days would begin when the Antichrist stops the daily sacrifice and would end at the conclusion of Armageddon. The prophet wrote, "And from the time that the daily sacrifice shall be taken away, and the abomination that maketh desolate set up, there shall be a thousand two hundred and ninety days" (Daniel 12:11). There is a difference of thirty days. It follows logically that the period of 1,290 days, which will end when the battle of Armageddon ends, must therefore begin thirty days prior to the time when the Antichrist will be assassinated, rise satanically from the dead, and then enter the Holy of Holies in the Temple. In other words, a significant prophetic event (the cutting off of the sacrifice) will occur thirty days prior to the midpoint of the seven-year Tribulation.

This prediction of Daniel 12:11 suggests that, during the terrible persecution of new Jewish and Gentile believers in the Messiah during the Tribulation period, the Antichrist will put an end to animal sacrifice on the Temple Mount thirty days before the midpoint of the Tribulation. It is possible that the Antichrist's stopping of the daily sacrifice may be the motivation for a Jewish believer to assassinate the Antichrist (see Revelation 13:3). The apostle John foretold that the Antichrist (the Beast) will be assassinated with a knife wound to his head or neck at the midpoint of the seven-year-long Tribulation period. John's prophecy also reveals that Satan will resurrect the assassinated Antichrist. During the first three and a half years of the Tribulation period, he will present himself to the world as a messiah figure who is an economic, political, and military genius. However, after his resurrection, he will claim to be God. The False Prophet (the satanically empowered partner of the Antichrist) will then demand that everyone on earth worship the resurrected Antichrist as God. "And he exerciseth all the power of the first beast before him, and causeth the earth and them which dwell therein to worship the first beast, whose deadly wound was healed" (Revelation 13:12).

An unusual revelation in Daniel 12 mentions that there is yet one more overlapping prophetic period, lasting 1,335 days, which will conclude with a special blessing of God to Israel during the coming millennial rule of the Messiah. "Blessed is he that waiteth, and cometh to the thousand three hundred and five and thirty days" (verse 12). While we can't be certain what the final blessing will be, it is entirely possible that the period of 1,335 days (beginning with the Antichrist's defilement of the Holy of Holies in the Temple) will end seventy-five days after the conclusion of the seven-year-long Tribulation and the battle of Armageddon (1,335 - 1,260 days = 75 days). Only the future fulfillment of this prophecy will reveal the final blessing that will be given to Israel and the Gentile nations when Jesus Christ returns to set up His millennial kingdom.

A Time Line for the "Time of the End"

Jesus promised that the last-days generation that witnessed the rebirth of Israel (May 1948) would also witness His return to earth to set up His messianic kingdom. Christ declared, "Now learn a parable of the fig tree; When his branch is yet tender, and putteth forth leaves, ye know that summer is nigh: so likewise ye, when ye shall see all these things, know that it is near, even at the doors. Verily I say unto you, This generation shall not pass, till all these things be fulfilled" (Matthew 24:32–34). This means that you and I are part of the last-days generation when "all these things be fulfilled."

The psalmist prophesied, "When the LORD shall build up Zion, he shall appear in his glory" (Psalm 102:16). "Zion" (Israel) has certainly been "built up" to an astonishing degree since 1948. The Bible uses the fig tree repeatedly as a prophetic symbol of the nation of Israel (Jeremiah 24:1–10; Hosea 9:10). We can confidently await the return of Christ in our lifetime. According to Psalm 90:10, the length of a typical lifetime or a natural generation is seventy to eighty years: "The days of our years are threescore years and ten; and if by reason of strength they be fourscore years." The most natural and logical interpretation of Christ's prophecy is that many of those who were alive in 1948 will live to see the fulfillment of the messianic prophecies regarding the "time of the end." Most people who were very young during Israel's 1948 War of Independence are still alive today. Many of this generation could see the fulfillment of Daniel's prophecies.

Because Daniel's prophecies are so detailed, it is already possible to see the fulfillment of some of his dreams and visions.

Knowledge Will Increase

The angel's command to Daniel was as follows: "Seal the book, even to the time of the end: many shall run to and fro, and *knowledge shall be increased*" (Daniel 12:4). No one has to tell us that this prophecy is being fulfilled every day. The rate of technological change has accelerated at an unprecedented rate.

If we look at technologies such as shipbuilding, engineering, weapons development, and general scientific knowledge, there was relatively little progress from the days of Rome until approximately the 1850s. The ships of Rome differed little in technology from the vessels used by the British navy during the Napoleonic Wars only two centuries ago. As late as the middle of the 1800s, physicians had virtually no knowledge of germs, and there was very little emphasis on hygienic techniques, even during surgery or childbirth. However, from the 1850s to 1900 the world witnessed an extraordinary explosion of scientific and technological knowledge in the fields of mechanical engineering, medicine, basic scientific research, and the development of new weaponry.

It has been estimated that the total of human knowledge probably doubled in the sixteen-plus centuries from the time of Jesus until the beginning of the Enlightenment in the seventeen hundreds. The last genius who was able to fully comprehend the totality of all scientific knowledge in his generation was probably Leonardo da Vinci, who died in 1519. However, in our modern generation it has become impossible for any individual, no matter how brilliant, to fully comprehend the total amount of knowledge now available regarding *even one* area of science, such as biology or metallurgy. Following the Enlightenment, the growth of scientific knowledge accelerated in the following century as the Industrial Revolution exploded with scientific advances that transformed virtually every aspect of life. It is estimated that today the sum total of human knowledge is doubling every two years.

As the growth of knowledge accelerates, every aspect of our lives is transformed. This includes education, work, social interactions, military conflicts, transportation, entertainment, and communications. Virtually each decade now reveals astonishing advances in *every* area of life. A significant measure of the growth of knowledge can be found in the massive increase in the issuing of patents. In the year 1900, the United States granted approximately 20,000 patents. By the end of World War II, the Patent Office was issuing 50,000 patents annually. In 1998, it was noted that "over 100,000" ideas were patented every year.[3] By February 2006, more than 7 million U.S. patents had been issued, with 443,652 patents filed in that year alone.[4]

The small nation of Israel, with a population of less than six million, is rated number three in the world in the issuing of patents.[5]

My Macintosh laptop exceeds the computational speed and memory storage capacity of the Cray supercomputer in 1976, which cost $8.8 million. Scientists are now building supercomputers and creating artificial-intelligence programs that are capable of modifying their own programming. These supercomputers will be able to design a next generation of computers that won't be fully comprehended by human scientists. IBM has completed its creation of possibly the fastest computer in the world, the

Blue Gene supercomputer, which can complete one million billion calculations every second. We are seeing the fulfillment of Daniel's prophecy that "knowledge shall be increased."

Travel Shall Increase

The second part of the angel's prophecy to Daniel was that at "the time of the end: many shall run to and fro" (Daniel 12:4). His prophecy indicated that both the quantity and the speed of travel would increase dramatically in the days leading to the coming again of the Messiah. Throughout thousands of years of recorded history, the vast majority of people never traveled more than thirty miles from the place they were born. Today it is common to travel that far just to go to work, and no one thinks it's unusual to travel to the other side of the globe on a business trip or a vacation.

The limited transportation technology available throughout the centuries preceeding World War I meant that the speed of travel was limited to approximately thirty-five miles per hour, the speed of a galloping horse or a ship under sail. However, in less than one hundred years, we don't even give thought to traveling six hundred miles per hour in a commercial jet. And astronauts orbit the Earth at a speed of more than eighteen thousand miles per hour.

TWO RESURRECTIONS AT THE END OF THE AGE

God revealed to Daniel that following the victory of the Messiah at the end of this age, the righteous and those wicked sinners who rejected God's offer of salvation through Christ's death will be resurrected. "And many of them that sleep in the dust of the earth shall awake, some to everlasting life, and some to shame and everlasting contempt" (Daniel 12:2). In the New

Testament, the Lord confirmed that there will be two separate resurrections. The first resurrection will include the righteous believers in God, both Old and New Testament believers, who will rise to eternal life in heaven. "Behold, I shew you a mystery; We shall not all sleep, but we shall all be changed, in a moment, in the twinkling of an eye, at the last trump: for the trumpet shall sound, and the dead shall be raised incorruptible, and we shall be changed" (1 Corinthians 15:51–52).

The second resurrection will involve unrepentant sinners who have chosen to reject Jesus and God's plan of salvation. "And I saw a great white throne, and him that sat on it, from whose face the earth and the heaven fled away; and there was found no place for them. And I saw the dead, small and great, stand before God; and the books were opened: and another book was opened, which is the book of life: and the dead were judged out of those things which were written in the books, according to their works. And the sea gave up the dead which were in it; and death and hell delivered up the dead which were in them: and they were judged every man according to their works. And death and hell were cast into the lake of fire. This is the second death. And whosoever was not found written in the book of life was cast into the lake of fire" (Revelation 20:11–15). Tragically, the unrepentant sinners will experience eternal separation from God in hell. Millions in our generation choose to believe that anyone who is sincere in his spiritual quest, regardless of his faith, will ultimately find salvation. However, the Word of God absolutely rejects this claim. The Scriptures declare that Jesus Christ is the only hope for humanity: "Neither is there salvation in any other: for there is none other name under heaven given among men, whereby we must be saved" (Acts 4:12).

The angel commanded Daniel to seal the vision to "the time of the end" (Daniel 12:4, 9). The clear implication is that the meaning of these prophecies would finally be unsealed as the time of the end approached. While unbelievers will never understand, genuine believers in God's Word will understand the prophecies of God about Christ's imminent return as the final crisis approaches.

Chapter 10

The Rise of the Antichrist

The Identifying Traits of Satan's Global Dictator

And the king shall do according to his will;
and he shall exalt himself, and magnify himself
above every god, and shall speak
marvellous things against the God of gods,
and shall prosper till the indignation be accomplished:
for that that is determined shall be done.

—DANIEL 11:36

M ORE THAN ANY OTHER OLD TESTAMENT PROPHET, Daniel had visions that were detailed and precise in their descriptions of Israel's future during the seven years of the Tribulation. Writing more than twenty-five centuries ago, Daniel saw the apocalyptic events that will unfold in our lifetime. By studying the Old and New Testament prophecies, we can discover the signs to look for that tell us the last days have begun. If you know which signs to read, you very quickly realize that many of the last-days prophecies are now being fulfilled, and many others will soon become visible.

For example, it's possible to document the first steps in the political maneuvering associated with the European Union's diplomatic and economic unification efforts. These developments are setting the stage for the

Antichrist's future global government. Based on the prophecies of Daniel chapter 12, we can plot an accurate time line for the Antichrist's rise to power, the major events during the seven-year Tribulation, and the battle of Armageddon.

Many readers have requested that I present a clear outline of the events that will unfold in our generation, from the time of Israel's rebirth as a nation in 1948 to Jesus Christ's return. Following is a chronological list of the major prophesied events of the last days.

A number of these prophecies warrant a closer look. The time line begins with the year 1948, when Israel once again became an independent nation. Jesus prophesied that in the last days the Jews would return to the land (see Matthew 24:32–34). Some of the other prophecies have yet to take place, although we can see a number of clear indications that several will be fulfilled in the very near future.[1]

In this chapter we will focus on three end-times developments. The first two—rapid climate change and the Mark of the Beast—are last-days prophecies for which the signs abound. Studying the third prophecy— regarding the character and nature of the Antichrist—will make us aware of Satan's plans for the world in this generation. In chapter 11 we will look in detail at the role of the Antichrist as his actions lead up to the battle of Armageddon, the final battle in which Satan will attempt to destroy God's people.

MASSIVE CLIMATE CHANGE

The scientific community has been debating the causes and extent of global climate change for two decades. It seems clear that we are in a long

THE PROPHESIED EVENTS OF THE LAST DAYS

MAJOR PROPHECY	BIBLICAL REFERENCE
1. The rebirth of Israel (the fig tree buds)	Matthew 24:32–34
2. Hebrew language is recovered	Zephaniah 3:9
3. The Jewish exiles return to Israel	Ezekiel 37:21
4. The desolate land becomes fertile	Isaiah 27:6
5. Plans to rebuild the Temple	Isaiah 2:2–3; Micah 4:1–2
6. The global rise of anti-Semitism	Matthew 24:9–10
7. Israel surrounded by enemy Arab nations	Psalm 83:4–8
8. The revival of the Roman Empire	Daniel 7:24–25
9. Development of worldwide communications	Revelation 11:9–10
10. Return of the Ethiopian Jews to Israel	Zephaniah 3:10

Major Prophecy	Biblical Reference
11. Russia rises again as a military power	Ezekiel 38:1–12
12. Babylon is rebuilt	Isaiah 13:1, 6, 19
13. Preparations for a one-world government	Daniel 7:14; Revelation 13:7
14. Financial systems will require the mark	Revelation 13:17–18
15. All must receive the mark	Revelation 13:16–18
16. Asia forms a 200-million-man army	Revelation 9:14–16
17. The Euphrates River will be dried up	Revelation 16:12–14
18. A military highway appears across Asia	Revelation 9:14–15; 16:12–14
19. Ecological devastation of the planet	Revelation 11:18
20. Massive climate change	Revelation 8:7–13
21. Humanity's survival threatened	Matthew 24:21–22; Joel 2:3

period of global warming. However, there is no scientific consensus on whether this can be traced to possible variations in solar radiation or to man-made causes. Scientific evidence does document that the average temperature on earth has increased during the last century. In addition, the level of the oceans is rising (approximately eight inches since 1900), and this trend will likely continue with potentially disastrous consequences to human populations. The Intergovernmental Panel on Climate Change, a United Nations organization, has noted that overwhelming evidence supports the theory that the earth will experience significant climatic change in the decades ahead.[2]

An increase in average global temperatures will produce major changes in the climate. Significant climate change would produce massive problems for humanity, posing an unprecedented challenge to governments that will be expected to protect their citizens and mitigate the negative effects of climate change.

Significantly, John prophesied such a crisis in the last days:

> The first angel sounded, and there followed hail and fire mingled
> with blood, and they were cast upon the earth: and the third part of
> trees was burnt up, and all green grass was burnt up. And the second
> angel sounded, and as it were a great mountain burning with fire was
> cast into the sea: and the third part of the sea became blood; and the
> third part of the creatures which were in the sea, and had life, died;
> and the third part of the ships were destroyed. And the third angel
> sounded, and there fell a great star from heaven, burning as it were a
> lamp, and it fell upon the third part of the rivers, and upon the foun-
> tains of waters; and the name of the star is called Wormwood: and

the third part of the waters became wormwood; and many men died of the waters, because they were made bitter. (Revelation 8:7–11)

In his vision John saw the unprecedented destruction of one-third of the world's vegetation, which will occur during the final seven years of this generation, leading to the return of Christ. Oceans and rivers will be poisoned, resulting in massive loss of aquatic life. Certainly, the worst possible scenarios presented by today's environmentalists regarding global climate change could not exceed the prophecies of the apostle John.

THE MARK OF THE BEAST

The book of Revelation describes a cashless society in the last days. In order to buy or sell, it will be necessary to possess a certain number, 666, which is the Mark and Number of the Beast (the Antichrist). This was an astonishing and improbable prophecy when John proclaimed it in the first century. How could one number be the key to allow a person to transact business, to obtain commodities, or to complete any financial transaction? Yet today the number of your credit-card account or debit-card account is essential to much of your buying and selling.

And he causeth all, both small and great, rich and poor, free and
bond, to receive a mark in their right hand, or in their foreheads:
and that no man might buy or sell, save he that had the mark, or
the name of the beast, or the number of his name. Here is wisdom.
Let him that hath understanding count the number of the beast:
for it is the number of a man; and his number is Six hundred threescore and six. (Revelation 13:16–18)

Already, North Americans live in a 97 percent cashless society. Less than 3 percent of the money in our economy exists as either paper currency or coins. John, in the book of Revelation, prophesies that the number 666 will be placed beneath the skin of people on the right hand or the forehead as a way to enforce people's allegiance to the Antichrist as their god and to control people throughout the Antichrist's world empire.

Such an invasive technology is not far from being reality. Companies are developing sophisticated technology that uses tiny radio-frequency identification chips, which could hold data and records on your complete identity. These chips could contain your biometric ID and your medical and financial records, and they are small enough to be placed beneath your skin. A miniature computer chip, the size of a large grain of rice, that can hold up to five gigabytes of information already exists. This chip could store as much information as is contained in thirty sets of the *Encyclopaedia Britannica*. Your complete financial, medical, legal, and personal records could easily be held in such an ID chip, and it could be accessed and read from a distance by electronic scanners. *Business Week* magazine reported that MasterCard International was testing a "smart card" computer chip that includes information about your private identity, including your fingerprints, and can be embedded in a credit card.[3]

The new VeriChip, a beneath-the-skin radio frequency chip, can be implanted and will contain comprehensive information about an individual, together with a GPS locator system that will allow an interested party or institution not only to locate an individual but to identify the person, along with his or her financial, medical, and even criminal records.[4] Already, certain card scanners used in stores and banks can scan your fingerprint and compare it to the information stored on certain credit cards as a way to prevent credit-card fraud and identity theft.

THE CHARACTERISTICS AND NATURE
OF THE ANTICHRIST

God went to great lengths to make sure His people would have the information they need to identify the Antichrist when he arrives on the world scene. In both the Old and New Testaments, the prophets used names and titles to characterize the Antichrist. These identifying names indicate his career, his nature, his goals and strategies, his agenda, and his ultimate defeat at the hands of the coming Messiah. Following are identifying marks of the Antichrist as found in Old Testament prophecies.

Satan's Seed: the Antichrist

"And I will put enmity between thee and the woman, and between thy seed and her seed; it shall bruise thy head, and thou shalt bruise his heel" (Genesis 3:15). The first prophecy in the Bible was made by God in the presence of Satan. God refers to the Antichrist as the seed of Satan because he will attempt to do the will of his father, Satan, who is the father of all lies. The prophecy of Genesis 3:15 describes the eternal hatred toward Christ that drives the work, strategies, and goals of Satan's seed.

The King of Babylon

"That thou shalt take up this proverb against the king of Babylon, and say, How hath the oppressor ceased! the golden city ceased!" (Isaiah 14:4). Isaiah called the Antichrist the "king of Babylon" because he will make the rebuilt city of Babylon one of his capitals. During the Antichrist's seven-year reign, Babylon will be a great Middle Eastern economic power. However, when the Antichrist is destroyed, Babylon will be burned.

The Little Horn

"I considered the horns, and, behold, there came up among them another little horn, before whom there were three of the first horns plucked up by the roots: and, behold, in this horn were eyes like the eyes of man, and a mouth speaking great things" (Daniel 7:8). Daniel called the Antichrist a "little horn," in contrast to the ten horns that represented the ten nations of the revived Roman Empire in the last days. Though endowed by Satan with supernatural powers, the Antichrist will still be a man until his assassination and satanic resurrection. He will be a powerful speaker, impressing people with his brilliant skills as a communicator.

A King of Fierce Countenance

"And in the latter time of their kingdom, when the transgressors are come to the full, a king of fierce countenance, and understanding dark sentences, shall stand up" (Daniel 8:23). The Antichrist will be a forceful leader, or "king," with "fierce countenance." Daniel's prophecy indicates that he will have a striking appearance and will possess great charisma. The phrase "when the transgressors are come to the full" reminds us that the fulfillment of these prophecies will not occur until man's sinful rebellion reaches the breaking point during the seven-year Tribulation period.

The Prince That Shall Come

"And after threescore and two weeks shall Messiah be cut off, but not for himself: and the people of the prince that shall come shall destroy the city and the sanctuary; and the end thereof shall be with a flood, and unto the end of the war desolations are determined" (Daniel 9:26). The unusual grammar of this prophecy reveals that the Antichrist will be a true "prince" who will rise to power and lead the revived Roman Empire of ten nations as a unified superstate. Daniel's prophecy of the "people [who]...shall destroy the city and the sanctuary" was initially fulfilled in AD 70 when the Roman armies (people) led by Prince Titus, the son of Emperor Vespasian, burned Jerusalem. Since Daniel's prophecy clearly declares that "the prince that shall come" will come out of the Roman people that destroyed "the city and sanctuary," the Antichrist will arise from and rule over the revived Roman Empire.

The Willful King

"And the king shall do according to his will; and he shall exalt himself, and magnify himself above every god, and shall speak marvellous things against the God of gods, and shall prosper till the indignation be accomplished: for that that is determined shall be done" (Daniel 11:36). In total contrast to Jesus, who came to do His Father's will (see John 6:38–39), Satan's Antichrist will "do according to his will." He will exalt his own sinful desires against all opposition until he is defeated by Jesus Christ at Armageddon.

The Assyrian

"Therefore thus saith the Lord GOD of hosts, O my people that dwellest in Zion, be not afraid of the Assyrian: he shall smite thee with a rod, and shall lift up his staff against thee, after the manner of Egypt" (Isaiah 10:24). While the Jewish prophets clearly identify the Antichrist as the one who will rule the Roman Empire in the last days, we are also told of his future connection with the Middle East and the rebuilt city of Babylon. Ancient Assyria occupied the same geographic area as Babylon prior to 608 BC. The prophecy of Isaiah 10:24 may identify the Antichrist symbolically by the name "the Assyrian" because of his future role in Babylon, the ancient territory of Assyria and a leading enemy of the Jewish people.

The Wicked

"With righteousness shall he judge the poor, and reprove with equity for the meek of the earth: and he shall smite the earth with the rod of his mouth, and with the breath of his lips shall he slay the wicked" (Isaiah 11:4). "And then shall that Wicked be revealed, whom the Lord shall consume with the spirit of his mouth, and shall destroy with the brightness of his coming" (2 Thessalonians 2:8). Both Isaiah and the apostle Paul described the Antichrist as the "wicked." He will give himself up entirely to Satan's possession, devoting himself to Satan's designs to destroy God's people. Despite the initial success of the Antichrist, the Messiah will destroy him at the battle of Armageddon "with the brightness of his coming."

THE ANTICHRIST AS DESCRIBED IN THE NEW TESTAMENT

The New Testament prophets warn about the terrible enemy of God who will oppress the believers who are alive during the Tribulation. While some New Testament prophets, such as Paul and John, frequently use the same titles for the Antichrist that the Old Testament prophets used, many of the names they apply to the Antichrist are new. The names and descriptions in the New Testament prophecies reveal more details about the Antichrist's rise to power. The New Testament prophets also warn of his worldwide reign of terror against all who refuse his satanic demand to be worshiped as God.

The Man of Sin and the Son of Perdition

"Let no man deceive you by any means: for that day shall not come, except there come a falling away first, and that *man of sin* be revealed, *the son of perdition;* who opposeth and exalteth himself above all that is called God, or that is worshipped; so that he as God sitteth in the temple of God, shewing himself that he is God" (2 Thessalonians 2:3–4). Paul tells us that the great day of the Lord will be preceded by the "falling away." Other prophecies warn about religious apostasy in the last days. The Antichrist will be revealed only at the appropriate time, after God removes His restraining power (the Holy Spirit) (see 2 Thessalonians 2:6–7). Paul calls the Antichrist the "man of sin" in contrast to Jesus, who is the Son of God.

The Bible calls the Antichrist the "son of perdition" because, as the "seed" of Satan, he is destined to kill many Tribulation saints, yet he will finally be destroyed by God. He is destined to perdition in hell, "the lake of fire," because of his great sin. Judas Iscariot, the betrayer of Jesus, was the other "son of perdition." In both cases, the Bible indicates that these individuals were (and will be) possessed by Satan.

Antichrist

"Little children, it is the last time: and as ye have heard that antichrist shall come, even now are there many antichrists; whereby we know that it is the last time.… Who is a liar but he that denieth that Jesus is the Christ? He is antichrist, that denieth the Father and the Son" (1 John 2:18, 22). The title Antichrist is most commonly used to describe the last great enemy of humanity. The name Antichrist clearly suggests that he will counterfeit and appear to emulate Jesus. In order to deceive men about his true identity, he will initially attempt to fulfill the Old Testament prophecies in order to meet the Jewish expectations of their coming Messiah. We need to remember that Jesus Himself warned that "many shall come in my name, saying, I am Christ" (Mark 13:6).

The First Beast

John wrote in the book of Revelation, "And I stood upon the sand of the sea, and saw a beast rise up out of the sea, having seven heads and ten horns, and upon his horns ten crowns, and upon his heads the name of blasphemy" (13:1). The Antichrist is identified as the first "beast" and is seen rising out of the sea. This sea represents the world of politics and possibly the Mediterranean Sea, which was surrounded by the nations of the ancient Roman Empire.

THE ANTICHRIST WILL COME IN HIS OWN NAME

Jesus gave this prophecy of the Antichrist: "I am come in my Father's name, and ye receive me not: if another shall come *in his own name*, him ye will receive" (John 5:43). Hundreds of prophecies in the Old Testament point to Jesus as the promised Messiah. Although He fulfilled these prophecies, spoke "with authority" (see Luke 4:36), and performed countless miracles (including raising people from the dead), most of the people living in Israel rejected His claims to be the prophesied Messiah. Christ's prophecy in John 5:43 warned that although they rejected He who had come in the name of His Father, the Jews living in the last days would accept, for a time, the Antichrist as their promised messiah.

At the "time of the end," the Antichrist will consolidate his power over government, politics, economics, and the military. He will control the world and the people of the world, to the extent that anyone who refuses to worship him as God will be executed. But still his power will be limited. Satan will empower his servant to rule the world for seven years, but Jesus Christ will return to earth to protect His chosen people. Christ will destroy the Antichrist in the final battle—the battle of Armageddon.

Chapter 11

The Countdown to Armageddon

The Signs That Point to the Final Battle of This Age

And he gathered them together into a place
called in the Hebrew tongue Armageddon.

—REVELATION 16:16

THE HISTORY OF THE ANCIENT BABYLONIAN EMPIRE, the first and the greatest of the four world empires, is far from complete. After disappearing beneath the sands of the Iraqi desert by the time of the Islamic conquest in the seventh century AD, Babylon will rise again to a place of world influence and power during the reign of the Antichrist.

After more than a thousand years of silence, the ruins of Babylon were discovered during the early years of the nineteenth century. Excavations in the last two centuries confirmed many of the historic details recorded in the book of Daniel. Thousands of inscriptions were found containing the names of Nebuchadnezzar and other monarchs of the ancient biblical past.

The prophecies of Isaiah and John reveal that Babylon will be rebuilt in the last days and will become a major world economic power. The Iraqi Department of Antiquities carried out major restoration work by order of President Saddam Hussein, who wanted to rebuild the city as a showcase of Iraq's past and future glory. Hussein devoted more than $2 billion to the effort. Once the new Iraqi government is able to fully govern the country and the nation's military is able to maintain order and peace, Iraq's oil reserves—almost as great as those of Saudi Arabia—will generate tremendous national wealth. Soon Iraq will begin to enjoy its prophetic destiny as an economic superpower in the Middle East. The rebuilt city of Babylon will become one of the three capitals of the future Antichrist, as indicated by one of his prophetic titles, the "king of Babylon" (Isaiah 14:4). The other capitals will be Rome and Jerusalem.

Isaiah foretold the final destruction of the rebuilt city: "And Babylon, the glory of kingdoms, the beauty of the Chaldees' excellency, shall be as when God overthrew Sodom and Gomorrah" (Isaiah 13:19). Babylon was conquered numerous times throughout its history, but it has never been destroyed by fire from heaven as were Sodom and Gomorrah (see Genesis 19). Therefore, Isaiah's prophecy must refer to Babylon's final destiny. Deep underneath the foundations of the city lies an enormous lake of bitumen and oil sludge that bubbles up through the sand during the summer months. God has already put in place the fuel needed to fulfill His prophecy of Babylon's final judgment and destruction. Isaiah prophesied that this destruction will occur at the end of the seven-year Tribulation period: "Howl ye; for the day of the LORD is at hand" (Isaiah 13:6).

In this chapter we continue our examination of the major developments and events to come during the "time of the end," as revealed by Daniel and other prophets. Of particular interest are the Jewish believers who will witness of the coming Messiah during the Tribulation and Satan's plans, goals, and method of operation in the world during the Antichrist's seven-year reign. We also will look at the role of the Antichrist as history leads up to the battle of Armageddon, the final battle to be waged on earth.

Jewish Believers Will Be Witnesses to the Coming Messiah

The Lord knows in advance how many people will accept Christ's offer of salvation. "Simeon hath declared how God at the first did visit the Gentiles, to take out of them a people for his name. And to this agree the words of the prophets; as it is written" (Acts 15:14–15). Just as a shepherd knows each of his sheep, the Lord knows the number and names of those who follow Him. In the book of Romans, we see a reference to the "fulness of the Gentiles." Paul wrote, "For I would not, brethren, that ye should be ignorant of this mystery, lest ye should be wise in your own conceits; that blindness in part is happened to Israel, until the fulness of the Gentiles be come in" (11:25). This expression refers to the complete number of believers that God will draw out from the Gentile nations to be part of His "royal priesthood" and "peculiar people" (see 1 Peter 2:9).

The fulness of the Gentiles will conclude the Age of Grace when all Christians are raptured by being removed to heaven. Then the Lord will once again call upon Israel to be a spiritual witness and a light to the nations during the seven-year Tribulation that will follow. The Jewish witnesses will include Elijah and Moses (see Revelation 11:3–13); the 144,000 witnesses, including 12,000 from each of Israel's twelve tribes (see Revelation 7:4–8); and millions of new Jewish believers. Despite terrible persecution and martyrdom, hundreds of millions "of all nations, and kindreds, and people, and tongues" will hear the witness that they proclaim about the coming Messiah (see Revelation 7:9). As a result, these hundreds of millions will become Tribulation saints (see Revelation 7:14–17).

THE WARS AGAINST THE ANTICHRIST

The prophet Joel (520 BC) sounded this warning: "Proclaim ye this among the Gentiles; Prepare war, wake up the mighty men, let all the men of war draw near, let them come up: beat your plowshares into swords, and your pruninghooks into spears" (Joel 3:9–10).

Following the Antichrist's initial victory over the ten nations of the revived Roman Empire and the nations allied with that empire (based on the expanded European Union), the armies of the Antichrist will be concentrated initially in Europe and the Middle East. In the final three and a half years of the Tribulation, with the world suffering under the brutal rule of the Antichrist, a series of wars will be unleashed. A number of nations will rebel against the tyranny of the Antichrist, and those nations will wage war against the Antichrist's armies.

Many devastating battles will be fought leading up to Armageddon. The king of the south (Egypt and her African allies) will attack the Antichrist's forces gathered in Israel. Then the king of the north (Russia, Turkey, Syria) will join the invasion by bringing their armed forces from the north in a lightning attack on the armies of the Antichrist. "At the time of the end shall the king of the south push at him: and the king of the north shall come against him like a whirlwind, with chariots, and with horsemen, and with many ships" (Daniel 11:40). However, the Antichrist will swiftly counterattack, annihilating the enemy armies from the north and the south. The forces of Satan's prince, the Antichrist, will decisively win the first round of the war against the armies of the king of the north and the king of the south.

The Antichrist will command the support of most of the Western nations, led by his inner circle of ten European and Mediterranean nations. He will consolidate his armies in Israel, moving his headquarters to the Mount of Olives opposite Jerusalem (see Daniel 11:45), knowing that the final war will be fought there. Daniel foretold, "He shall enter also into the glorious land, and many countries shall be overthrown: but these shall escape out of his hand, even Edom, and Moab, and the chief of the children of Ammon. He shall stretch forth his hand also upon the countries: and the land of Egypt shall not escape" (Daniel 11:41–42). Edom, Moab, and Ammon in present-day Jordan will somehow escape. It is possible that they will willingly ally themselves with Satan's prince. The Antichrist will conquer Libya and Ethiopia as his armies consolidate his control over North Africa (see Daniel 11:43).

The Armies from the East

The nations of the eastern world (see the reference to the "kings of the east," Revelation 16:12–14) will unite in a desperate attempt to secure their political freedom by attacking the Antichrist's armies. Enormous armies of a size never seen before in human history will arise from several nations in Asia. These armies will march westward toward the Middle East, where they will engage in a cataclysmic struggle with the western armies of the Antichrist. An alliance between Japan, China, India, and the developing nations of Asia could produce the armaments and manpower for such an unprecedented army from the East.

The prophet John wrote, "I saw three unclean spirits like frogs come out of the mouth of the dragon, and out of the mouth of the beast, and out of the mouth of the false prophet. For they are the spirits of devils, working miracles, which go forth unto the kings of the earth and of the whole world, to gather them to the battle of that great day of God Almighty.... And he gathered them together into a place called in the Hebrew tongue Armageddon" (Revelation 16:13–14, 16). These satanic spirits will call the "kings of the earth" to gather their massive armies to march toward Israel to engage in the final conflict of the age against the armies of the Antichrist.

The Antichrist will receive intelligence reports that an enormous army is mobilizing far to the east and north in Asia. "But tidings out of the east and out of the north shall trouble him [the Antichrist]: therefore he shall go forth with great fury to destroy, and utterly to make away many. And he shall plant the tabernacles of his palace between the seas in the glorious holy mountain; yet he shall come to his end, and none shall help him" (Daniel 11:44–45). These reports will create a disturbance because the huge army of the kings of the east will contain two hundred million soldiers (see Daniel 11:40–44; Revelation 9:16).

Naturally the number of soldiers mentioned (two hundred million) astonished John and his readers because the population of the entire Roman Empire in the first century was nowhere near this number. Indeed, the world's *entire population* at that time was approximately two hundred million people.[1]

At no time in ancient history was a nation, or even a large confederation of nations, capable of raising an army numbering two hundred million men. But in our last-days generation, it is entirely possible. The total population of the nations of Asia is approximately three billion. With China having inadvertently encouraged the birth of sons through government directives, including its One Child policy, the kings of the east will have more than enough men of military age to join such a massive force. China already maintains the world's largest standing army of almost three million soldiers, plus one million reservists and fifteen million militia.

A staggering increase in the number of male children resulted from China's One Child policy, which in a short time could produce in the population an imbalance of males numbering in the tens of millions. Chinese couples often abort baby girls in the hope of having a son later on. The preponderance of male children in Asia has been enhanced by millions of couples in India who want male heirs and also want to avoid the expense of paying dowries to marry off daughters. So, similar to couples in China, many Indian couples abort female babies.

The Western world will face its final crisis when the military brilliance, the technology, and the engineering accomplishments of Japan are joined to the huge manpower and natural resources of China and India. China and India are rapidly expanding their nuclear arsenals while building military alliances with Iran, Pakistan, Saudi Arabia, Syria, and Algeria. Both China and North Korea are providing sophisticated intermediate ballistic missiles and advanced nuclear technology to many Middle Eastern enemies of the West, including Iran and Syria.

The Military Highway from Asia

For a world war to take place, massive numbers of troops, vehicles, equipment, and armaments will have to be transported to the Middle Eastern battlefield. In the book of Revelation, John refers to a military highway of the kings of the east that will allow the two-hundred-million-man army to travel from the Far East to northern Israel (see Revelation 16:12). The Chinese government has spent extraordinary sums of money to build an unprecedented highway from mainland China across Tibet and southern

Asia, heading west toward the Middle East. This military highway through the most rugged mountain terrain has no obvious economic purpose, and no foreigners are allowed near it. The following (poorly translated) statement regarding this highway, from an article by Oleg Limanov in *Marco Polo Magazine,* reads, "Karakorum highway, connecting Afghanistan through Central Asia states and China to Pakistan with probable joining India would be very significant for all concerning parties, agreement on using of which was signed by China, Pakistan, Kazakhstan and Kyrgyzstan in July 1996."[2]

Another article describes the land route from China toward the Middle East: "With Myanmar [Burma] support, the Indian government is creating a transportation corridor from South Asia through Myanmar to Southeast Asia. This corridor will compete with other grand trans-Eurasian projects, such as a land transportation link from China through Central Asia to Turkey and Europe."[3]

THE DEADLIEST WEAPONS EVER USED IN WAR

The weapons used in the battle of Armageddon will be the most destructive ever employed in the history of warfare. Jesus warned that only His return to earth at the conclusion of the battle of Armageddon would make it possible for humanity to survive. Advanced weapons technology now being developed will be unleashed in the cataclysmic wars at the end of this age. The United States, Britain, Russia, China, and Israel have designed advanced neutron atomic bombs that will kill every living creature within an eight-city-block area without damaging buildings or equipment.

Russia and China have killer satellites equipped with lasers capable of destroying American surveillance satellites that allow our military commanders to observe military operations around the world. (During the invasion of Iraq in 2003, sophisticated satellite cameras transmitted pictures of live battles back to the War Room in the Pentagon, allowing military commanders and political leaders to observe individual enemy vehicles and enemy combatants in battle in real time.) In response to the threat of killer satellites, America has created a series of sophisticated backup satellites that orbit in deep space. They can be activated if our first set of satellites is destroyed. The replacement satellites will descend to the proper orbit to observe and report any new military conflict.

Israel has developed several high-energy plasma beam (the fourth state of matter) weapons that will revolutionize warfare. The Israelis did not use these advanced weapons in the 2006 war in Lebanon because they knew the danger from Hezbollah was limited to conventional weapons systems such as Katusha rockets.

Despite denials, the Russians have spent billions on the development of particle-beam weapons as well as weapons that use sound waves that can destroy soldiers or vaporize a hard target from great distances. A single particle-beam or laser-beam weapon can be aimed at hundreds of targets per minute, destroying them at the speed of light with the power of a tactical nuclear weapon.[4]

As we approach the end of this age, the combined military manpower of the world's standing armies and reserves exceeds five hundred million soldiers. More than eighty-five thousand nuclear weapons and huge stockpiles of biological and chemical weapons are stored in armories around the world. Older weapons are often sold to countries such as Egypt, who then sell their twenty-year-old military equipment to poorer nations such as Yemen. There are enough military arms throughout the world to supply every human on the planet with a weapon.

The nations of the world spend more than one trillion dollars annually for armaments. Students of prophecy realize there is an explanation for the nations' obsession with arms and armies. The growing preparations for war are moving inexorably toward the last war of the age, the battle of Armageddon.

Genetic Weapons That Target Particular Races

I have spent more than forty years researching political, military, and intelligence matters involving countries all over the world. I have concentrated the majority of my study on the nations of the Middle East, but one piece of data disturbs me more than anything else I have uncovered.

The remarkable DNA discoveries in recent years, resulting in mapping the incredibly complex human genetic code, have now been extended to the development of genocidal weapons systems. Such weapons can target a particular ethnic or racial group for death. Who would have imagined that scientific advances in genetics would further the development of diabolical weapons of mass destruction? Data generated by genetic research is being perverted to develop a new class of weaponry that will target limited populations of victims. These weapons are similar to the more familiar biological weapons that use disease-causing spores, bacteria, and other pathogens. However, this new class of weapons will use DNA to select victims based on race. Scientific programs are under way in several nations (including Russia, China, and South Africa) to develop diseases that would attack members of a defined enemy race while leaving members of the aggressor nation's population unaffected.

These developments are so horrifying that I have refrained from sharing my research on this subject for several years. A report on findings released by the British Medical Association (BMA) carries this sobering message: "Advances in genetic knowledge could be misused to develop powerful biological weapons that could be tailored to strike at specific ethnic groups, the British Medical Association has warned. A BMA report [entitled] Biotechnology, Weapons and Humanity says that concerted international action is necessary to block the development of new, biological weapons. It warns the window of opportunity to do so is very narrow as technology is developing rapidly and becoming ever more accessible. 'Recipes' for developing biological agents are freely available on the Internet, the report warns."[5]

Unfortunately, genetic research is now so advanced that even morally responsible nations, such as the United States and Israel, have been forced to develop defensive research programs in an attempt to protect their national populations from genetic weapons. Think about the terrible conflict that the Bible warns will occur in the final years of this age, leading to the battle of Armageddon and Christ's return. In light of the genocidal potential of DNA weapons, we begin to understand why Jesus declared, "And except those days should be shortened, there should no flesh be saved: but for the elect's sake those days shall be shortened" (Matthew 24:22). Fortunately, Jesus will supernaturally intervene during the battle of Armageddon to prevent the utter destruction of human populations.

The Asian Armies Will Cross the Euphrates

For thousands of years the Euphrates River has stood as a military barrier between east and west. The river runs for more than a thousand miles from its headwaters in the mountains of Turkey. It flows south through the territory of ancient Babylon until it empties into the Persian Gulf. Its width varies from a few hundred feet to more than a mile. John foretold that this great river will someday dry up to allow the army of the east to march across Asia toward northern Israel. John prophesied, "And the sixth angel poured out his vial upon the great river Euphrates; and the water thereof was dried up, that the way of the kings of the east might be prepared" (Revelation 16:12).

During the 1980s and 1990s, Turgut Ozal, Turkey's president, built a series of twenty-two dams on the Tigris and Euphrates river systems. The huge Atatürk Dam, the fifth-largest dam on earth, is part of the $32 billion Southeastern Anatolia Project, which was designed to produce electricity and to double the irrigation capacity to approximately thirty thousand square miles of semiarid land. This series of dams is intended to allow Turkey to produce ample food for the growing population of the Middle East. The Atatürk Dam is estimated to provide irrigation to more than four million acres of land, enabling Turkish farmers to grow cotton, tobacco, sugar beets, and soybeans.

What is most notable about the Atatürk Dam, which is more than a mile long and six hundred feet high, is that it is capable of blocking the headwaters of the Euphrates River. In 1990, at the opening of the dam, the president of Turkey pressed a button, the dam closed, and the water level in the Euphrates dropped by 75 percent. Never before in history had this been possible. The great Euphrates River can now be dried up, exactly as prophesied by John, to allow an Asian army to march toward Israel across the battlefields of ancient Mesopotamia. This army will destroy untold millions as it marches across Asia. A voice from heaven declared, "Loose the four angels which are bound in the great river Euphrates. And the four angels were loosed, which were prepared for an hour, and a day, and a month, and a year, for to slay the third part of men. And the number of the army of the horsemen were two hundred thousand thousand: and I heard the number of them" (Revelation 9:14–16).

THE LAST BATTLE

The two-hundred-million-man army of the kings of the east will fight its way across Asia as it travels to do battle with the huge western military forces of the Antichrist, mobilized in the Valley of Jezreel in northern Israel. This final battle between the kings of the east and the armies of the Antichrist will determine who will rule the world. However, the total defeat of both armies will establish the government of Jesus Christ during the next thousand years.

The battle of Armageddon will be focused on the large plain known as the Valley of Jezreel in northern Israel. The name Armageddon ("the mount of Megeddo") is derived from the ancient city of Megiddo, a fortified city built by King Solomon. The city's ruins lie on a plateau overlooking the enormous valley. Throughout the history of Israel, more than a dozen critical battles have been fought here, including the defeat of the armies of Judah and the death of King Josiah. Significantly, when the conqueror Napoleon visited this battleground in 1800, he remarked with a general's viewpoint that "all the armies on earth could maneuver their forces on this vast plain."[6]

Although the final stages of this battle will take place in northern Israel, the war will engulf all of Asia, North Africa, Europe, and the Middle East. Hundreds of millions will die as the advanced weapons systems now being developed will be put into use by both east and west to slaughter enemy armies. Nothing will be held back as nations seek the total destruction of their enemies' armies and cities. A full-scale nuclear, biological (perhaps genetic), and chemical war will destroy massive numbers of the armies and the civilian populations of the countries attacked.

John described the final phase of the battle of Armageddon as the armies will engage in desperate pitched battle against one another and, naturally, against the armies of Israel that will valiantly attempt to defend its people. To the amazement of the leaders of these warring armies, Jesus Christ and the armies of heaven will intervene against all the enemies of God's chosen people. John wrote, "I saw the beast, and the kings of the earth, and their armies, gathered together to make war against him that sat on the horse, and against his army" (Revelation 19:19). The forces of the nations of the entire planet will then attack the armies of heaven. The armies of the Antichrist and the kings of the east will be utterly destroyed by Christ's supernatural power. The resurrected Christians in their new bodies will return from heaven with their Messiah to join in His victory over the armies of east and west. John foretold that "the armies which were in heaven followed him [Jesus] upon white horses, clothed in fine linen, white and clean" (Revelation 19:14).

Both the Old and New Testaments foretell the return of the hundreds of millions of resurrected saints of the church on the day the Messiah will establish His kingdom. The first prophet to appear in the Bible, Enoch, predicted that the Lord will bring millions of His saints with Him on the Great Day of the Lord. "Behold, the Lord cometh with ten thousands of his saints" (Jude 14). The expression "ten thousands" means "ten thousand times ten thousand," which equals one hundred million. Moses also described the Lord and His heavenly army coming from Sinai to take vengeance against Satan's forces: "The LORD came from Sinai, and rose up from Seir unto them; he shined forth from mount Paran, and he came with ten thousands of saints: from his right hand went a fiery law for them" (Deuteronomy 33:2).

THE ULTIMATE VICTORY OF THE LORD

The battle of Armageddon may end very quickly once Jesus Christ and the armies of heaven intervene, or it may rage on for some time. There is some hint of this in that the prophet Zechariah tells us that Christ will destroy the remnant of the armies of the Antichrist some days later as they attempt a final assault on Jerusalem. The prophet declared, "Behold, the day of the LORD cometh, and thy spoil shall be divided in the midst of thee. For I will gather all nations against Jerusalem to battle; and the city shall be taken, and the houses rifled, and the women ravished; and half of the city shall go forth into captivity, and the residue of the people shall not be cut off from the city. Then shall the LORD go forth, and fight against those nations, as when he fought in the day of battle" (Zechariah 14:1–3).

Regardless of the duration, the ultimate victory of the heavenly armies of Christ is assured. The apostle Paul prophesied, "And then shall that Wicked be revealed, whom the Lord shall consume with the spirit of his mouth, and shall destroy with the brightness of his coming" (2 Thessalonians 2:8). Daniel also referred to the supernatural defeat of the Antichrist: "He shall also stand up against the Prince of princes; but he shall be broken without hand" (8:25). When Christ was betrayed, He indicated the vast power that was available to Him as the Son of God: "Thinkest thou that I cannot now pray to my Father, and he shall presently give me more than twelve legions of angels?" (Matthew 26:53). When the final day of reckoning comes, Christ will call on His legions of angels as well as the millions of resurrected saints in their indestructible bodies to join in His triumphant return to earth.

John describes the destiny of the global dictator, the Antichrist, and his partner, the False Prophet: "And the beast was taken, and with him the false prophet that wrought miracles before him, with which he deceived them that had received the mark of the beast, and them that worshipped his image. These both were cast alive into a lake of fire burning with brimstone. And the remnant were slain with the sword of him that sat upon the horse, which sword proceeded out of his mouth: and all the fowls were filled with their flesh" (Revelation 19:20–21).

WELCOMING THE KINGDOM OF GOD

I have spent decades studying prophecy and comparing it with current world events, and I am convinced we are rapidly approaching the final events leading to the Apocalypse—the rise of the Antichrist with his world government and the return of Jesus Christ to set up His kingdom. While many people view prophecy as a message of "doom and gloom," I don't see it that way at all. While humanity is approaching a seven-year period of trial and tribulation unequaled even in World War II, the hopeful message of Bible prophecy is that humanity will survive and that Christ's victory over Satan's Antichrist will usher in the greatest period in the history of mankind: the kingdom of God. In God's kingdom, peace, justice, and righteous government will exist for the first time since the Garden of Eden.

Jesus spoke to His disciples regarding the appropriate response to the fulfillment of these prophecies: "And then shall they see the Son of man coming in a cloud with power and great glory. And when these things begin to come to pass, then look up, and lift up your heads; for your redemption draweth nigh" (Luke 21:27–28).

Jesus Christ, the Messiah, is coming back to redeem the world!

Answering the Critics of the Book of Daniel

No other book of the Bible has sustained more severe, or more constant, attacks on its authenticity and credibility than the book of Daniel. The reason for this is simple: the book of Daniel provides the most convincing and comprehensive evidence that proves the divine inspiration of Scripture, the identification of Jesus as the Messiah, and the accuracy of the many prophecies concerning the events leading up to Christ's return.

When reading the future through the visions of an Old Testament prophet, there are always those who cast doubt on the authenticity of the prophecies. The book of Daniel has been under attack for centuries from liberal theological scholars and philosophers who have lost their faith in the inspired Word of God, God's supernatural intervention in the world, His miracles, the incarnation of Jesus Christ, His resurrection, and especially in the spiritual phenomenon of God's prophetic revelations regarding future historical events. These anti-supernatural critics deny the authenticity of the book of Daniel as well as its supernatural authority as part of the inspired revelation of God.

While the details of the attacks vary, they ultimately depend on the rejection of the possibility that God possesses knowledge of the future and that He transmits that knowledge to humanity through prophets. More than a century ago, Dr. Edward B. Pusey, a great scholar of Daniel's prophecies, identified the fundamental issues to be determined by any serious inquiry regarding the book of Daniel. "It is either divine or an imposture. To write any book under the name of another, and to give out to be his, is, in any case, a forgery, dishonorable in itself and destructive of all trustworthiness.... The writer, were he not Daniel, must have lied on a most frightful scale."[1]

Porphyry, a pagan critic of Christianity in the third century, ironically argued against Daniel's prophecy based on the specificity and accuracy of the predictions. The prophecies were so precise that Porphyry declared that Daniel's writing must have been written *after* the historical events occurred. Porphyry (c. AD 285) claimed that the book of Daniel was not written around 540 BC as Daniel claimed but rather that it was composed as a fraudulent prediction around 165 BC, after the oppression of King Antiochus Epiphanes and his defeat by the Jewish rebels. Porphyry claimed that Daniel's book was created by an unknown writer to encourage the Jews in their life-and-death struggle with the Syrians in 168–165 BC. But numerous references to the prophecies of Daniel appear in documents that were written *long before* the Maccabean Jewish revolt against Antiochus Epiphanes. (King Antiochus Epiphanes ruled 175–164 BC.)

The Greek Septuagint translation of the Old Testament is, in itself, proof that Daniel's writing predates 165 BC. The Septuagint ("Seventy") was translated in 285 BC by seventy Jewish scholars in Egypt under the direct orders of Ptolemy Philadelphus, king of Egypt. This translation of the Old Testament Scriptures includes the prophecies of Daniel and was produced more than a century *before* the reign of Antiochus Epiphanes. The inclusion of the book of Daniel in the Septuagint Bible provides unassailable proof that Daniel's book was in existence and universally accepted by the Jews as part of the Word of God at least 120 years before 168 BC. In addition, the Jewish sages who compiled the various books into the canon of the Hebrew Bible accepted the book of Daniel as genuine Scripture in approximately 406 BC.

The book of Daniel contains specific predictions that were fulfilled *after* the Septuagint was translated but prior to the modern argument of the critics of Daniel's authenticity. Included among these is the precise time that the Messiah was "cut off," a prophecy that was fulfilled exactly as predicted on Palm Sunday AD 32. This was some two centuries *after* the date that early critics alleged the "fraudulent" book of Daniel was written.

THE LEADING ARGUMENTS THAT SUPPORT DANIEL

Daniel's prophecies have been proven to be historically accurate, which leaves us with only two logical explanations: either the book of Daniel records supernatural prophecy from God or it is a fraud.

Daniel claims that he recorded these prophecies prior to 536 BC. That means his prophetic book contains tremendously accurate descriptions of events that occurred centuries *after* Daniel's death. The second possible conclusion is that the prophecies are frauds, produced by an impostor writing about events long after they occurred. The author then presented them as ancient biblical "prophecies" around 168 BC.

Critics who reject the authenticity of Daniel's prophecies often do so without seriously considering the historical and textual evidence that supports its authenticity. The historical and textual evidence prove that the book of Daniel was written by the prophet Daniel more than five centuries before Christ. Therefore, the book of Daniel presents genuine prophecies that were inspired by God and fulfilled just as they were predicted. Many of the prophesied events were fulfilled long after 168 BC, which is the date that most critics assign to the book, assuming an impostor described the events after the fact.

We dare not ignore the prophecies of Daniel that are such a central part of God's whole counsel to His church in the last days. A careful examination of the historical, archaeological, linguistic, and biblical evidence proves categorically that the book of Daniel is genuine, inspired prophecy composed before 536 BC. In past centuries Jewish sages and the leaders of the early church who lived much closer to the time of the Babylonian captivity agreed that the prophecies of Daniel were legitimate.

In the mid-1800s, skeptics began rejecting the idea that Daniel's prophecies were genuine. They had concluded that predictive prophecy and the supernatural are simply impossible. The argument of the critics against the early biblical date (606 BC to 536 BC) for the writing of Daniel's prophecy is untenable in the face of the historical and manuscript evidence.

The greatest danger to the faith of Christians does not come from external attacks by openly declared enemies of the gospel and the church. The real danger comes from pastors who have already lost their personal confidence in the "faith which was once delivered unto the saints" (Jude 3). In his excellent defense of the authenticity of Daniel's prophecies, Edward B. Pusey wrote, "The faith can receive no real injury except from its defenders.... If the faith shall be (God forbid!) destroyed in England, it will not be by open assailants, but by those who think they defend it, while they themselves lost it."[2]

We need to understand the secret motives of many who deny the inspiration of the book of Daniel as well as those who declare that Daniel's prophecies must have been written by an impersonator who adopted the name Daniel in 168 BC, after most of the "predicted" events had taken place. These critics usually reached their conclusion long before they considered the historical or textual evidence. The critics' anti-supernatural thinking is as follows: genuine prophecy is impossible; therefore, a book containing accurate predictions of events that would occur hundreds of years in the future must have been written *after* the events occurred. Professor Pusey correctly pointed out the true origin of their criticism: "They overlooked the historical point that the disbelief had been antecedent [previous] to the criticism. Disbelief had been the parent, not the offspring of their criticism."[3]

For those who will examine the evidence objectively, it's easy to see that the evidence overwhelmingly supports the early date of 606 BC to 538 BC, centuries *before* the events he prophesied actually occurred.

The Prophet Ezekiel

Ezekiel, a prophet who was a contemporary of Daniel and also living as a Jewish exile during the Babylonian captivity, was aware of the exalted position of his fellow Jew, who had risen to become prime minister of the pagan empire. Ezekiel referred to Daniel's prophecies and accepted Daniel's status as one of God's true prophets.

Ezekiel wrote his prophetic book in Babylon around 550 BC and referred to Daniel three times in two separate passages. In the first passage, Ezekiel records that God declared that a land that persistently sinned against Him would be punished though these three men, "Noah, Daniel, and Job, were in it" (Ezekiel 14:14, 20). Then in Ezekiel 28, Ezekiel relates how God described Satan before he fell into rebellion and sin. Ezekiel wrote, "Behold, thou [Satan] art wiser than Daniel; there is no secret that they can hide from thee" (verse 3). In light of these inspired references to Daniel almost four centuries before 168 BC, it almost defies understanding how a serious scholar could believe the book of Daniel was composed by an anonymous impostor some four hundred years later.

The Books of Maccabees

In the historical book 1 Maccabees in the Apocrypha, written approximately 110 BC, the author recounted the history of Mattathias and his sons' heroic battle for the defense of their Jewish faith against Antiochus Epiphanes (168–165 BC) and the establishment of the Hasmonean dynasty in Israel. The author reminds readers of the great heroes in Israel's history, referring to Daniel and his three friends' unshakable faith. "Ananias, Azarias, and Misael, by believing were saved out of the flame. Daniel for his innocency was delivered from the mouth of lions" (1 Maccabees 2:59–60). These statements provide the strongest possible evidence that the writer, who was familiar with the Maccabees and the Jewish rebellion, was also familiar with Daniel's writings and believed the prophet's account was historically accurate.

Three Greek Words in the Text of Daniel

Some critics have rejected the authenticity of Daniel on the basis that three Greek words for musical instruments appear in Daniel's text. The critics believe that Greek words would not have made their way into a book written in Babylon two centuries before the time of Alexander the Great's conquest of the Middle East. However, this criticism has now generally been abandoned due to historical evidence that there were many contacts and much trade between Greece and Babylon in Daniel's time.

Christ's References to Daniel's Prophecies

The evidence from Scripture that confirms the authority of Daniel as a prophet of God is overwhelming. Jesus quoted from Daniel's prophecies, giving the book of Daniel and the prophet himself the highest validation possible.

On the Mount of Olives Jesus declared, "When ye therefore shall see the abomination of desolation, spoken of by Daniel the prophet, stand in the holy place, (whoso readeth, let him understand:) then let them which be in Judaea flee into the mountains" (Matthew 24:15–16). In this prophetic declaration, Jesus directly affirmed that Daniel was a true prophet of God and thereby confirmed the authority of Daniel's prophecies. In addition, our Lord commanded Christians to read and understand the words of Daniel's prophecy. Later, Jesus made another clear reference to one of Daniel's prophecies: "Thou hast said: nevertheless I say unto you, Hereafter shall ye see the Son of man sitting on the right hand of power, and coming in the clouds of heaven" (Matthew 26:64). This recalled the prophecy in Daniel 7:13: "Behold, one like the Son of man came with the clouds of heaven."

God Creates and Preserves His Chosen People

Remarkably, the Jewish nation is the only nation that can reliably trace its origin to one single human. Jews, Muslims, and Christians all agree that Abraham is the father of the Jewish people.

There is a clear logic to the Bible's account of God's choice of Israel to be the people through whom He would provide His divine revelation to all of humanity. It was essential to choose a man who would father a new people, a nation that had never before existed. When God decided to create a people of His own, a new nation, He selected a man who did not rule a kingdom or even occupy a country. God created a people descended from Abraham. They had no country, so God directed them to travel toward a relatively unoccupied area in Palestine on the shore of the Mediterranean.

There is a fascinating quote in the book *The Amazing Jew* by A. J. Pollock regarding the unique nature and survival of the Jewish people.

"Inhabitants of Babylon and Memphis would have found it hard to believe that out of their imperial pomp the only living relics would be the utterances of an obscure tribe upon their frontiers; that Nebuchadnezzar's name would be lost to all except archeologists, but for its mention in the Hebrew Scriptures."[1]

Famous American author Mark Twain wrote of the Jew: "His contributions to the world's lists of great names in literature, science, art, music, finance, medicine, and abstruse learning are also away out of all proportion to the weakness of his numbers. All things are mortal but the Jew; all other forces pass, but he remains. What is the secret of his immortality?"[2]

The astonishing record of the Jews' survival throughout the last four thousand years provides compelling evidence of the finger of God in human history. Madison C. Peters had this to say in his book *The Jew as a Patriot:* "The Jew has given to the world the knowledge of the only true and living God. He has given Moses, whose laws still form the basis of the civilized world's jurisprudence; Jesus, the ideal of the race.... Of whom Strauss [David Strauss, Bible critic, 1838] said, 'He remains the highest model of religion within our thoughts.'"[3]

Peters quotes Dr. Max Nordaw, who spoke of Jesus in the following terms: "Who could think of excluding Him from the people of Israel?... 'This Man is ours, He honors our race, and we claim Him as we claim the Gospels—flowers of Jewish literature, and only Jewish!' Our Bible, the Old as well as the New Testament, was written by Jews."[4]

And what does God declare regarding His choice of the Jews as His chosen people?

Who are Israelites; to whom pertaineth the adoption, and the glory, and the covenants, and the giving of the law, and the service of

God, and the promises; whose are the fathers, and of whom as concerning the flesh Christ came, who is over all, God blessed for ever. Amen. (Romans 9:4–5)

And the scripture, foreseeing that God would justify the heathen [the Gentiles] through faith, preached before the gospel unto Abraham, saying, In thee shall all nations be blessed. So then they which be of faith are blessed with faithful Abraham. (Galatians 3:8–9)

For thou art an holy people unto the LORD thy God: the LORD thy God hath chosen thee to be a special people unto himself, above all people that are upon the face of the earth. The LORD did not set his love upon you, nor choose you, because ye were more in number than any people; for ye were the fewest of all people: but because the LORD loved you, and because he would keep the oath which he had sworn unto your fathers, hath the LORD brought you out with a mighty hand, and redeemed you out of the house of bondmen, from the hand of Pharaoh king of Egypt. (Deuteronomy 7:6–8)

God created Israel to bless all the Gentiles on earth. After more than 400 years of oppression and captivity in both Canaan and Egypt—and the subsequent 40 years spent wandering in the Sinai wilderness—Joshua led the chosen people across the Jordan River to establish a nation in Canaan. For the next 450 years, Israel was governed by judges appointed by God. However, Israel rejected God's governmental and judicial system and demanded a king to replace the judges, in keeping with the kings who ruled the surrounding Gentile nations. The Lord allowed Israel to have its monarchy, but He warned that eventually this system would lead to national disaster. Their first king, Saul, instituted high taxes, a standing army, and the tyranny that God had warned about.

After the righteous reign of King David, Israel began to sink into idolatry under David's son Solomon, who married hundreds of pagan women and produced unrighteous descendants. Solomon's unfaithfulness escalated to the point that he introduced pagan idols into the Temple in Jerusalem (see 1 Kings 11:1–7). After Solomon's death, the nation of Israel split into two kingdoms—the southern kingdom of Judah under Solomon's son Rehoboam, and the northern kingdom of Israel under Jeroboam. At that point God brought judgment on Israel by using Gentile empires to punish His unfaithful people. Several centuries of rebellion, coups, and unrighteous leadership followed, until the people of the northern kingdom of Israel and later the southern kingdom of Judah were taken captive. Jeremiah had warned the leaders of Judah that the land would be conquered by the rising Babylonian Empire.

GOD'S CHOSEN PEOPLE IN EXILE

The ancient Jews believed that, as the chosen people, the Lord would never allow them to be conquered by a pagan empire, regardless of their spiritual rebellion. However, God warned them repeatedly that the sin of worshiping false gods would bring terrible consequences.

In 607 BC Jeremiah came to the royal court in Jerusalem, where ambassadors from the nations surrounding Israel were gathered. The prophet wore a yoke around his neck as a symbol of slavery, and God later placed the pagan nations surrounding Israel under the yoke of the Babylonian Empire. Jeremiah announced to this powerful assembly: "Thus saith the LORD of hosts,…now have I given all these lands into the hand of Nebuchadnezzar the king of Babylon, my servant; and the beasts of the field have I given him also to serve him. And all nations shall serve him, and his son, and his son's son, until the very time of his land come" (Jeremiah 27:4, 6–7). The prophecy warned that God, in response to Israel's spiritual rebellion, was transferring control of the Promised Land from Israel to the Babylonian Empire. The rising empire of Babylon would exercise supremacy over the nations, but only for seventy years.

In 608 BC Babylon rose to world power and was destroyed exactly seventy years later (in 538 BC) by the Medo-Persian Empire of King Darius. Two years after the beginning of the Babylonian Empire, in the spring of 606 BC, Prince Nebuchadnezzar conquered the land of Judah and her new king, Jehoiakim. Nebuchadnezzar transported thousands of aristocratic and noble captives, including Daniel, six hundred miles east to Babylon, the capital city (see 2 Kings 24:1–2; Daniel 1:1). Babylon, which had been a southern province of the ancient Assyrian Empire, took advantage of the weakened leadership of Assyria's last king to launch a brilliant attack that conquered the Assyrian capital of Nineveh in 610 BC, exactly as the Old Testament prophets had foretold.

THE KINGDOM OF ASSYRIA

For several centuries prior to this, the kingdom of Assyria had been attacking Israel. The Assyrian army was the most brutal the world had yet seen. Its standard practice included skinning captives alive and cutting off the noses, thumbs, and toes of prisoners of war, even captured kings. Assyria conquered most of the Middle East under a series of powerful kings. Shalmaneser II fought Israel's King Ahab in 853 BC, and Tiglath-pileser III carried some of the Jewish people into captivity. The Assyrian kings

Shalmaneser IV and Sargon II completed the destruction of the northern kingdom of Israel during the reign of the Jewish king Hoshea. Assyria destroyed the northern kingdom's capital, Samaria (in today's West Bank), in 721 BC.

However, long before the time of Tiglath-pileser III, the Assyrian armies of Sennacherib conquered the city of Babylon. Esarhaddon and Ashurbanipal dominated the province of Babylon despite its continued rebellion against Assyria. For two hundred years, from the eighth century BC until the sixth century BC, Babylon gradually declined in power, becoming a regional administrative center under the authority of Assyria. Many of the Assyrian kings just named are recorded in the Bible's history of the Assyrian invasions of the Holy Land.

Despite Assyria's overwhelming power, God's prophets warned that Assyria and its capital, Nineveh, were doomed to certain destruction. In obedience to God's command, the reluctant prophet Jonah traveled to Nineveh during the early part of the eighth century BC. Jonah warned of the coming destruction unless the Assyrians repented of their wickedness and idolatry. Jonah warned, "Yet forty days, and Nineveh shall be overthrown" (Jonah 3:4). In the most marvelous miracle recorded in the Old Testament, the entire population of Nineveh—from king to slave—repented and confessed their sins to God. As a result of their national repentance, God postponed His judgment. However, almost a century later Nineveh reverted to its pagan ways and was destroyed.

By 626 BC the empire of Assyria fell into political and military disarray. A powerful provincial Chaldean ruler named Nabopolassar proclaimed himself king of the Assyrian province of Babylonia. Later he defeated the demoralized Assyrian armies and then destroyed Nineveh. From that time,

Babylon became the center of political and military power in the known world for seventy years.

THE FALL OF BABYLON

Cyrus, the new king of Persia, was foretold *by name* by Isaiah a century and a half before he rose to power. He conquered the Babylonian Empire in 538 BC. King Cyrus, as recorded in 2 Chronicles 36:23, issued his remarkable decree in 536 BC that commanded the freedom and release of the various captive populations, including the Jews, that were scattered throughout the recently conquered Babylonian Empire. This was a huge area that today is occupied by Syria, Iraq, Iran, and Afghanistan. Exactly seventy years after the beginning of the Babylonian captivity and two years after Babylon was overthrown by Media-Persia, the Jews were allowed to return to Israel. "The LORD stirred up the spirit of Cyrus king of Persia, that he made a proclamation throughout all his kingdom.... Who is there among you of all his [God's] people? The LORD his God be with him, and let him go up" (2 Chronicles 36:22–23). The decree releasing the captive peoples has been recovered by archaeologists. I have seen this clay cylinder that contains the text of King Cyrus's decree, which is on display in the British Museum in London. The archaeological evidence confirms the accuracy of the biblical account of this historic decree.

But in spite of King Cyrus's decree allowing the Jewish exiles to return to Israel, the books of Ezra and Nehemiah reveal that less than 1 percent of the exiles from the ten northern tribes (the kingdom of Israel) and less than 5 percent of the captives from the two southern tribes (the kingdom of Judah) took advantage of the Persian king's offer to return to Jerusalem.

The vast majority of the Jews living in Babylon had integrated into the thriving commerce of the wealthy empire, settling into a comfortable life-style. After seventy years, the vast majority of Jews living in Babylon had been born in exile and had no memory of the Promised Land.

Historical records from the time of Christ suggest that up to ten mil-lion Jews were then living in the Gentile lands far to the east of Jerusalem. Fascinating historical references have been traced of Jews who entered China from Afghanistan in ancient times, as well as Jewish gravestones whose names suggest they are descended from the ten northern tribes of Israel. These gravestones, dated hundreds of years before Christ, were located north of the Black Sea in present-day Russia.

Communities of exiled Jews in central Asia produced rich Jewish reli-gious literature, including the Babylonian Talmud. The religious influence of these Jewish communities created fertile ground for the spread of the Christian gospel in central Asia during the first-century missionary jour-neys of early apostles such as Bartholomew and Thomas.

GOD PRESERVED HIS PEOPLE

Jewish communities spread throughout the vast Persian Empire (120 provinces) were endangered by Haman, who attempted to carry out a plan of genocide as recorded in the book of Esther. There is an interesting but little-known aspect to God's miraculous deliverance of the Jews at that time. The Jewish queen Esther intervened with her Gentile husband, King Xerxes. God raised up Queen Esther to save the Jews at that critical moment in history. Years later the Jewish cupbearer, Nehemiah, a senior court official and valued counselor to the Persian king Artaxerxes, appeared before the king. When the king asked why was he depressed, Nehemiah

This clay cylinder contains the text of King Cyrus's decree that allowed the captive Jews to return to Israel.

requested that he be allowed to return to Jerusalem to rebuild the walls and gates of the burned city.

The Scriptures declare that more than 42,360 Jews returned to Judah in 536 BC to rebuild their houses. In 520 BC they finished rebuilding the Temple, but the people lacked the leadership and the will to rebuild the walls of Jerusalem. Surprisingly, Artaxerxes allowed Nehemiah to lead a mission of Jews back to Judah to rebuild the city walls. The king also provided him with a great amount of materials to complete the task.

Have you ever wondered why the pagan king of the Persian Empire, the most powerful empire at that time, responded so willingly to Nehemiah's request? The answer will surprise you: the Persian king Artaxerxes was actually a Jew!

One day while comparing chronological records with the biblical accounts concerning ancient Mideast empires, it struck me that King Artaxerxes was not really the Gentile king of Persia but rather he was a Jewish king as defined by Jewish law, the son of the Jewish queen Esther. Esther was apparently referred to in the Persian records by her Persian name, Amestris. Artaxerxes was the son of the great Persian king Xerxes, who died in 465 BC. The biblical account in Nehemiah 2:1 declares that the decree allowing the rebuilding of Jerusalem was signed in the twentieth year of King Artaxerxes (445 BC). He was undoubtedly taught the love of God and developed a profound concern for the Jews at his mother's knees. God used Esther's spiritual obedience to save her people from Satan's genocidal attack during the days of Haman. However, God allowed her marriage to King Xerxes to produce a Jewish son, Prince Artaxerxes, who would later, as the king of Persia, play a key role in God's plans to restore Jerusalem and Israel.

The decree to rebuild the city walls was signed the first day in the Jewish month of Nisan (March 14) 445 BC (the twentieth year of King

Artaxerxes' reign), as foretold in Daniel's prophecy: "Know therefore and understand, that from the going forth of the commandment to restore and to build Jerusalem unto the Messiah the Prince shall be seven weeks, and threescore and two weeks" (Daniel 9:25). The royal decree, issued March 14, 445 BC, began the period of sixty-nine weeks of Daniel's vision. Daniel's reference to the Messiah being "cut off" was fulfilled to the exact day on Palm Sunday AD 32 (see 9:26), when Jesus was rejected by the leadership of Israel (see Luke 19:37–44).

GOD'S PEOPLE, CHOSEN TO BLESS
THE PEOPLE OF THE WORLD

God created a people for Himself. He decided to use His chosen people to bless the Gentile nations. He chose as the father of this nation the man Abraham, whom He commanded to leave his home and to travel to the land of Canaan. God created a nation of His own out of one man, not out of an existing kingdom.

As we move nearer to the last days, God will bless all nations through the Jewish people in a way that has never before been seen on earth. Israel's Messiah will return to establish His kingdom on earth after He delivers Israel from the final assault of Satan's Antichrist. Once again, God's chosen people will be the focus of God's plan to bless humanity through the prophesied return of Jesus Christ the Messiah.

Notes

Introduction

1. Henry Fynes Clinton, *Fasti Hellenici*, 3 vols. (Oxford: Oxford University Press, 1835), 1:328.

Chapter 1

1. Ethirajan Anbarasan, "Genetic Weapons: A 21st-Century Nightmare?" *UNESCO Courier*, March 1999, www.unesco.org/courier/1999_03/uk/ethique/txt1.htm.
2. Aureleus Augustine, *On the Proceedings of Pelagius*, vol. 5, *Nicene and Post-Nicene Fathers*, ed. Philip Schaff (Grand Rapids: Eerdmans, 1978), 189.
3. Jerome, quoted in Gleason L. Archer Jr., *Jerome's Commentary on Daniel* (Grand Rapids: Baker, 1958), 15.

Chapter 2

1. Flavius Josephus, *The Antiquities of the Jews*, in *Josephus: Complete Works*, trans. William Whiston (Grand Rapids: Kregel, 1974), 227.
2. Isaac Newton, *Observations upon the Prophecies of Daniel, and the Apocalypse of St. John* (Lampeter, Dyfed, UK: Edwin Mellen Press, 1999), chap. 3, p. 1.
3. Evidence of this emphasis comes through clearly in the Dead Sea Scrolls.

4. The article on Daniel in *Smith's Bible Dictionary* declares, "There can be no doubt that it [the book of Daniel] exercised a greater influence upon the early Christian Church than any other writing of the Old Testament." See "Daniel," in *Smith's Bible Dictionary*, ed. William Smith (Boston: D. Lothrop, 1884), 132.

5. Josephus, *The Antiquities of the Jews*, 222.

6. According to the Jewish scholar Louis Ginzberg, both the Jewish Haggadah and the Chronicon Syriacum 27 declared that Bar Hebraeus, a bishop of the Syriac Orthodox Church in Persia in the thirteenth century, asserted that Daniel was also a descendant of King Jeconiah (Jehoiachin) of Judah. Louis Ginzberg, *The Legends of the Jews* (Philadelphia: Jewish Publication Society of America, 1968), 414.

7. James H. Charlesworth, *Apocalyptic Literature and Testaments*, vol. 1, *The Old Testament Pseudepigrapha* (New York: Doubleday, 1983), 821.

8. Josephus, *The Antiquities of the Jews*, 222.

9. Alfred E. Edersheim, *The Temple* (London: Religious Tract Society, 1912), 28.

10. The Jewish historian Flavius Josephus documented Nebuchadnezzar's taking of captives to Babylon. Josephus wrote, "He…came, and ordered the captives to be placed as colonists in the most proper places of Babylonia." See Flavius Josephus, *Against Apion*, in *Josephus: Complete Works*, trans. William Whiston (Grand Rapids: Kregel, 1974), 613.

11. The Greek historian Herodotus gives us an indication of the grandeur of the city of Babylon: "The temple of Jupiter Belus had

gates of brass; it was four hundred and forty yards on every side, and was foursquare. In the midst of the temple was a solid tower, two hundred and twenty yards in length and breadth; upon which another temple was placed." See Herodotus, *The History of the Persian Wars*, vol. 4, *The History of Herodotus*, trans. George Rawlinson (London: John Murray, 1875), 302.

12. Herodotus, *History of the Persian Wars*, 298.

Chapter 3

1. Herodotus, *The History of the Persian Wars*, vol. 4, *The History of Herodotus*, trans. George Rawlinson (London: John Murray, 1875), 53–74.

2. "And they burnt the house of God, and brake down the wall of Jerusalem, and burnt all the palaces thereof with fire, and destroyed all the goodly vessels thereof. And them that had escaped from the sword carried he away to Babylon; where they were servants to him and his sons until the reign of the kingdom of Persia: to fulfil the word of the LORD by the mouth of Jeremiah, until the land had enjoyed her sabbaths: for as long as she lay desolate she kept sabbath, to fulfil threescore and ten years" (2 Chronicles 36:19–21).

3. Robert Anderson, *The Coming Prince* (Grand Rapids: Kregel, 1969), 221.

4. Herodotus, *History of the Persian Wars*, 312.

5. See Flavius Josephus, *The Antiquities of the Jews*, in *Josephus: Complete Works*, trans. William Whiston (Grand Rapids: Kregel, 1974), 244.

Chapter 4

1. George Rawlinson, "Dura," in *Smith's Bible Dictionary*, ed. William Smith (Boston: D. Lathrop, 1884), 154.

2. Albert Barnes, *Notes on the Book of Daniel* (New York: Leavitt & Allen, 1855), 273. The monuments were discovered by Capt. Robert Mignan of the East India Company a century and a half ago.

Chapter 5

1. Flavius Josephus, *The Antiquities of the Jews*, in *Josephus: Complete Works*, trans. William Whiston (Grand Rapids: Kregel, 1974), 225.

2. Jose ben Halafta, *Seder Olam Rabbah*, chap. 28, AD 160.

Chapter 6

1. By the time Daniel reported on his vision depicting four great beasts, the prophet's written record had diverged from the historical chronology of events in Babylon. The events described in Daniel chapter 7 occurred *prior* to the historical events reported in Daniel 5 and 6. However, the first section of Daniel's book of prophecy (chapters 1 through 6) deals mostly with historical events. The second section (chapters 7 through 12) deals primarily with prophetic matters. The prophet placed his vision of the four beasts within the second, prophetic section.

Chapter 7

1. The story of the Maccabean Revolt is told in the deuterocanonical books 1 and 2 Maccabees.

Chapter 8

1. H. Freedman and Maurice Simon, eds., and Maurice Simon, trans., *Midrash Rabbah: Genesis,* vol. 1, *Bereshit Rabba* (London: Soncino Press, 1939), sec. 93, fol. 84.4.

2. Hugh Grotus, *De Veritate Religionis Christianae* [On the Truth of the Christian Religion] (Paris, 1627), sec. 14.

3. Hersh Goldwurm, *Daniel,* ArtScroll Tanach Series (Brooklyn: Mesorah, 1979), 260.

4. Goldwurm, *Daniel,* 260.

5. *Encyclopaedia Britannica,* 6th ed., s.v. "chronology."

6. *Encyclopaedia Britannica,* 6th ed., s.v. "chronology."

7. Herbert Danby, trans., *Mishna, Rosh Hashanah* (New York: Oxford, 1983), note on p. 102.

8. Robert Anderson, *The Coming Prince* (Grand Rapids: Kregel, 1969), 124.

9. Flavius Josephus, *Wars of the Jews,* in *Josephus: Complete Works,* trans. William Whiston (Grand Rapids: Kregel, 1974), 565.

10. Irenaeus, *Against Heresies,* vol. 1, *The Ante-Nicene Fathers,* ed. Alexander Roberts (Grand Rapids: Eerdmans, 1980), 566.

11. Hippolytus, *Hippolytus, Cyprian Caius, Novatian,* vol. 5, *The Ante-Nicene Fathers,* ed. Alexander Roberts (Grand Rapids: Eerdmans, 1980), 248.

12. Shlomo ben Yitzchak, *Daniel: A New Translation with a Commentary,* ed. Nosson Scherman and Meir Zlotowitz (Brooklyn: Mesorah Publications, 1980), 226.

13. Yitzchak, *Daniel,* 261.

14. Talmud, *Yoma* 21b (London: Soncino Press, 1938), 94.

15. It is significant that archaeologists have discovered a flask containing the ancient oil of anointing near the Dead Sea in a cave described in the Copper Scroll. See my book *The New Temple and the Second Coming* (Colorado Springs, CO: WaterBrook, 2007), 56–58.

16. *Epistle of Barnabas,* vol. 1, *The Ante-Nicene Fathers,* ed. Alexander Roberts and James Donaldson (Grand Rapids: Eerdmans, 1987), 137.

17. Details about this discovery of the ancient Christian teaching of the pre-Tribulation Rapture can be found in my book *Triumphant Return* (Toronto, Ontario: Frontier Research, 2001).

18. Ephraem the Syrian, *The Cave of Treasures,* trans. E. A. Wallis Budge (London: Religious Tract Society, 1927), 235.

19. Ephraem the Syrian, *The Cave of Treasures,* 268–70.

20. David B. Barrett, *World Christian Encyclopedia,* 2nd ed. (Oxford: Oxford University Press, 2001), 3–6.

Chapter 9

1. This was prophesied by Ezekiel (see Ezekiel 4:4–6). For more on the return of the Jewish exiles to Israel, see my book *Armageddon* (Colorado Springs, CO: WaterBrook, 1997, 2004), 33–42.

2. Moses Maimonides, *Mishneh Torah* (Jerusalem: Moznaim Publishing, 1987).

3. Rich Donaldson, quoted by Lisa M. Whitley, "Great Ideas Turn into Palatable Investments," *Dallas Business Journal,* March 6, 1998.

4. "Number of Patents Issued," Invention Statistics, www.invention statistics.com/Number_of_New_Patents_Issued.html/.

5. "The Israeli VC Success Story," Vertex Venture Capital www.reseau capital.com/Conferences/Congres_2005/Oron%20Vertex.pdf, p. 7.

Chapter 10

1. If you would like to explore in detail the prophecies regarding the rebuilding of the Temple (see Isaiah 2:2–3; Micah 4:1–2), see my book *The New Temple and the Second Coming* (Colorado Springs, CO: WaterBrook, 2007).
2. This conclusion is based on data from the Intergovernmental Panel on Climate Change, found at www.ipcc.ch/.
3. *BusinessWeek*, June 3, 1996, 123.
4. "VeriChip Is I.D.'d as a Winner," *BusinessWeek*, May 28, 2007, http://tinyurl.com/4wkl3/.

Chapter 11

1. An estimate taken from the United States Census Bureau, "Historical Estimates of World Population," www.census.gov/ipc/www/worldhis.html/.
2. Oleg Limanov, "Central Asian Strategy of China: Political Containment or Economic Involvement," *Marco Polo Magazine*, January 1999.
3. "New Routes Across Asia?" AIG online, www.aig.com/Home.
4. G. Bekefi, B. T. Feld, J. Parmentola, and K. Tsipis, "Particle Beam Weapons—A Technical Assessment," *Nature* 284, March 20, 1980, 219–25.
5. "Genetic Weapons Alert," BBC News, 21 January 1999, http://news.bbc.co.uk/2/hi/health/259222.stm/.
6. Philologos, http://philologos.org/bpr/files/a005.htm/.

Appendix A

1. Edward B. Pusey, *Daniel the Prophet* (Plymouth, UK: Devonport Society, 1864), 1.
2. Pusey, *Daniel the Prophet*, 25.
3. Pusey, *Daniel the Prophet*, 6.

Appendix B

1. A. J. Pollock, *The Amazing Jew* (London: Central Bible Truth Depot, 1940), 9.
2. Mark Twain, "Concerning the Jews," *Harper's Magazine*, September 1899, 527–35.
3. Madison C. Peters, *The Jew as a Patriot* (Grand Rapids: Baker & Taylor, 1902).
4. Max Nordaw, quoted in Peters, *The Jew as a Patriot*.

Selected Bibliography

Anderson, Robert. *The Coming Prince*. Grand Rapids: Kregel, 1969.

Archer, Gleason L., Jr. *Jerome's Commentary on Daniel*. Grand Rapids: Baker, 1958.

Auerbach, Leo. *The Babylonian Talmud: In Selection*. New York: Philosophical Library, 1944.

Barnes, Albert. *Notes on the Book of Daniel*. New York: Leavitt and Allen, 1855.

Baylee, Joseph. *The Times of the Gentiles*. London: James Nisbet, 1871.

Besant, Walter, and E. H. Palmer. *Jerusalem*. London: Chatto and Windus, 1908.

Blackstone, William E. *Jesus Is Coming*. London: Fleming H. Revell, 1908.

Boutflower, Charles. *In and Around the Book of Daniel*. Grand Rapids: Kregel, 1977.

Budge, Wallis E. A. *Babylonian Life and History*. London: Religious Tract Society, 1925.

Bultema, Harry. *Commentary on Daniel*. Grand Rapids: Kregel, 1992.

Butterfield, Herbert. *Christianity and History*. New York: Charles Scribner and Sons, 1949.

Culver, Robert Duncan. *Daniel and the Latter Days*. Chicago: Moody, 1977.

Cummings, John. *Lectures on the Book of Daniel.* Philadelphia: Lindsay and Blakiston, 1855.

Davidson, John. *Discourses on Prophecy.* London: John Murray, 1825.

Dimont, Max I. *Jews, God and History.* New York: New American Library, 1962.

Edersheim, Alfred E. *Bible History: Old Testament.* Grand Rapids: Eerdmans, 1982.

———. *The Temple.* London: Religious Tract Society, 1912.

Eisemann, Moshe. *Ezekiel: A New Commentary Anthologized from Talmudic, Midrashic and Rabbinical Sources.* New York: Mesorah, 1980.

Eusebius. *Eusebius' Ecclesiastical History.* Edited by E. Burton. Translated by E. Burton and A. C. McGiffert. Oxford: Clarendon Press, 1881.

Fruchtenbaum, Arnold G. *The Footsteps of the Messiah.* San Antonio: Ariel Ministries, 1982.

Gaebelein, A. C. *The Prophet Daniel.* New York: Publication Office "Our Hope," 1911.

Gaster, Theodor H. *Festivals of the Jewish Year.* New York: Morrow Quill Paperbacks, 1953.

Gill, Stephen. *American Hegemony and the Trilateral Commission.* Cambridge: Cambridge University Press, 1990.

Hawley, Charles A. *The Teaching of Apocrypha and Apocalypse.* New York: Association Press, 1925.

Jones, Alexander, ed. *The Jerusalem Bible.* Garden City, NY: Doubleday, 1968.

Josephus, Flavius. *The Antiquities of the Jews.* In *Josephus: Complete Works.* Translated by William Whiston. Grand Rapids: Kregel, 1974.

———. *Wars of the Jews.* In *Josephus: Complete Works.* Translated by William Whiston. Grand Rapids: Kregel, 1974.

Kellogg, Samuel. *The Jews or Prediction and Fulfillment.* New York: Anson D. F. Randolf, 1883.

Larkin, Clarence. *The Book of Daniel.* Philadelphia: Clarence Larkin, 1929, 1949.

Lockyer, Herbert. *All the Messianic Prophecies of the Bible.* Grand Rapids: Zondervan, 1973.

Ludwigson, R. *A Survey of Bible Prophecy.* Grand Rapids: Zondervan, 1951.

Montgomery, James A. *The Book of Daniel.* In *The International Critical Commentary.* New York: Charles Scribner and Sons, 1964.

Newton, Isaac. *Observations upon the Prophecies of Daniel, and the Apocalypse of St. John.* Lampeter, Dyfed, UK: Edwin Mellen Press, 1999.

Payne, J. Barton. *Encyclopedia of Biblical Prophecy.* Grand Rapids: Baker, 1980.

Pentecost, Dwight. *Things to Come.* Grand Rapids: Dunham, 1958.

Peters, George. *The Theocratic Kingdom.* Grand Rapids: Kregel, 1957.

Peters, Joan. *From Time Immemorial: The Origins of the Arab-Israeli Conflict over Palestine.* New York: Harper and Row, 1984.

Pusey, Edward B. *Daniel the Prophet.* Plymouth, UK: Devonport Society, 1864.

Roberts, Alexander, ed. *The Ante-Nicene Fathers.* 10 vols. Grand Rapids: Eerdmans, 1988.

Robinson, Thomas. *The Preacher's Homiletic Commentary on the Book of Daniel.* Grand Rapids: Baker, 1881.

Sale-Harrison, L. *The Remarkable Jew.* London: Pickering and Inglis, 1928.

Scherman, Nosson. *Daniel: A New Commentary Anthologized from Talmudic, Midrashic and Rabbinical Sources.* New York: Mesorah, 1980.

Siegel, Richard, and Carl Rheins. *The Jewish Almanac.* New York: Bantam, 1980.

Tregelles, S. P. *Remarks on the Prophetic Visions in the Book of Daniel.* London: Sovereign Grace Advent Testimony, 1965.

Ussher, Jacob. *Chronology of the Old and New Testaments.* Green Forest, AR: Master Books, 2004.

Walvoord, John F. *Daniel: The Key to Prophetic Revelation.* Chicago: Moody, 1971.

Wright, Charles H. H. *Studies in Daniel's Prophecy.* Minneapolis: Klock and Klock Christian, 1983.

Zimmermann, Felix H. *Daniel in Babylon.* Broadview, IL: Gibbs, 1970.

Zlotowitz, Meir. *Bereishis (Genesis): A New Translation with a Commentary Anthologized from Talmudic, Midrashic and Rabbinic Sources.* New York: Mesorah, 1980.

About the Author

GRANT R. JEFFREY is the author of twenty-five books, including *The New Temple and the Second Coming, The Next World War, Surveillance Society, Armageddon,* and *The Signature of God.* He also is the editor of the *Marked Reference Prophecy Study Bible.* His decades of study in the areas of prophecy, history, theology, and archaeology are reflected in his books, which have been translated into twenty-four languages and have sold more than seven million copies throughout the world. His popular television program, *Bible Prophecy Revealed,* is broadcast twice weekly on Trinity Broadcasting Network. He also appears frequently as a guest on television and radio.

Jeffrey's passion for research has led him to acquire a personal library of more than seven thousand books on prophecy, theology, and biblical archaeology. He earned his master's degree and a Doctor of Philosophy in Biblical Studies from Louisiana Baptist University. Before becoming a full-time writer, he was a professional financial planner for eighteen years with his own brokerage company in western Canada.

ALSO BY GRANT R. JEFFREY

Apocalypse
Armageddon
Creation
Finding Financial Freedom
The Handwriting of God
Heaven
Jesus
The New Temple and the Second Coming
The Next World War
Prince of Darkness
The Signature of God
Surveillance Society
Triumphant Return
Unveiling Mysteries of the Bible
War on Terror

Available in bookstores and from online retailers.

WATERBROOK
PRESS

www.waterbrookpress.com

Don't miss these prophetic titles from Grant Jeffrey!

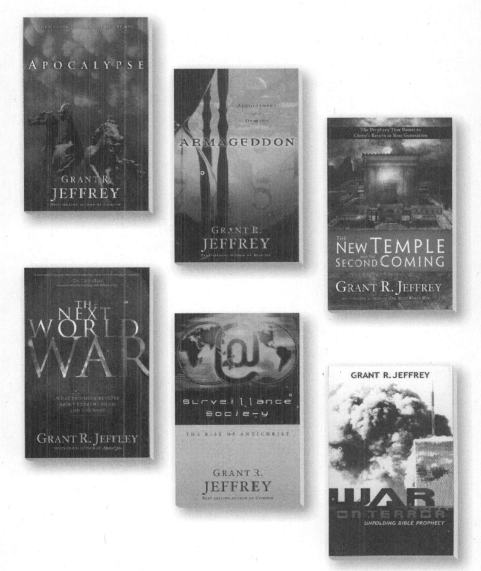